PROPERTY MANAGEMENT

Property Management

Corporate Strategies, Financial Instruments and the Urban Environment

MARK DEAKIN
School of the Built Environment,
Napier University

ASHGATE

Published by
Ashgate Publishing Limited
Gower House
Croft Road
Aldershot
Hants GU11 3HR
England

Ashgate Publishing Company
Suite 420
101 Cherry Street
Burlington, VT 05401-4405
USA

Ashgate website: http://www.ashgate.com

British Library Cataloguing in Publication Data
Deakin, M. (Mark), 1955-
    Property management : corporate strategies, financial
    instruments and the urban environment
    1. Real estate management - Finance 2. City planning -
    Economic aspects 3. Sustainable development - Economic
    aspects
    I. Title
    658.2

Library of Congress Cataloging-in-Publication Data
Deakin, Mark.
    Property management : corporate strategies, financial instruments and the urban
    environment / Mark Deakin.
        p. cm.
    Includes bibliographical references and index.
    ISBN 0-7546-3628-3
    1. Real estate management. 2. Real estate management--Environmental aspects. 3. Real
estate investment--Finance. 4. Real property--Valuation. 5. City planning--Environmental
aspects. 6. Land use, Urban--Environmental aspects. 7. Sustainable development. I. Title.

    HD1394.D427 2004
    333.33'068--dc22

                                                                              2004048252

ISBN 0 7546 3628 3

Printed and bound in Great Britain by
Athenaeum Press Ltd., Gateshead, Tyne & Wear

Contents

List of Figures

List of Tables

Chapter 1

Introduction

This book examines the development of property management in terms of the corporate strategies and financial instruments made use of to appraise the land and buildings making up the urban environment. The examination takes place under the following headings:

- Introduction
- Property Management
- Corporate Strategies
- Financial Instruments
- Computer-based Information Systems, Property Management and the Appraisal of the Urban Environment
- Sustainable Urban Development: the Framework and Directory of Environmental Assessment Methods
- Valuation, Investment Appraisal, Discounting, Obsolescence and Depreciation: their Impact on the Urban Environment
- Evaluating the Development of Sustainable Communities
- Conclusions

The chapters

The chapter on property management begins by outlining the issues underlying the development of property management. Under the heading of: value for money, economy, efficiency and effectiveness, attention is drawn to corporate strategies and financial instruments of property management. From here the text examines the corporate strategies developed to improve the standards of property management. The book then goes on to examine the financial instruments that have also been developed to bring about better standards of property management.

Having set out the corporate strategies and financial instruments of property management, the examination goes on to focus on one of the most pressing issues facing property management. Under the heading of 'computer-based information systems, property management and the appraisal of the urban environment', attention is drawn to how the said corporate strategies and financial instruments provide the capital accounting systems, asset registers and valuation methodologies needed to undertake a comprehensive appraisal of the land and buildings making up the urban environment. This examination shows that while a great deal of information is currently available on the various initiatives underlying the development of property management, there is still a noticeable absence of any data on either the corporate strategies, financial instruments, or computer-based information systems forming the mainstay of the capital accounting systems, asset registers and valuation methodologies under consideration.

The text

The text aims to close the gap that currently exists in what is understood about the development of property management, by providing academics, middle managers, directors and chief executives with the information required to not only manage property as a corporate resource, but make sure the strategies which are made use of for such purposes are financially sound. Developing this theme, the text goes on to examine the contribution capital accounting systems, asset registers and valuation methodologies make to sustainable urban development (SUD). Here the text provides a framework for analysing SUD and a directory of the environmental assessment methods currently available to appraise land and buildings. Examining the assessment methods under the heading of 'valuation and investment appraisal', the text goes on to study the impact discounting; obsolescence and depreciation have on the urban environment. This study is then drawn upon to show how the discounting mechanism is being used to develop sustainable communities. Following this conclusions are drawn and a research agenda is advanced.

The research projects

The examination draws upon a number of research projects the author has been engaged on over the past five years and is targeted at 'property managers' responsible for developing the corporate strategies and financial instruments (capital accounting systems, asset registers and valuation methodologies) needed to provide a comprehensive appraisal of the land and buildings making up the urban environment. The research projects in question include the following:

- The development of property management
- Financial services for the development of property management
- Sustainable urban development

The findings of these research projects have been published elsewhere (see Deakin, 1996; 1997a, b; 1998a; 1999a; Deakin 2000a, b, 2002a; Deakin and Curwell, 2002). The object of this book is to bring the body of work carried out to examine the development of property management together under one title. This is done under the heading of property management and qualified in terms of the corporate strategies and financial instruments underlying the developments in question. Taking a multi-disciplinary approach to the development, the publication brings together two disciplines (property management and environmental science) which have previously remained separate fields of study.

The first five chapters focus attention on the development of property management. Here attention is drawn to the corporate strategies, financial instruments and computer-based information systems underlying the development of property management. However, it is also here – with the development of computer-based information systems – that the common ground underlying the development begins to emerge. This emerges with the corporate strategies and financial instruments needed to provide a comprehensive appraisal of the land and buildings making up the urban environment. The common ground between property management and environmental science develops further in chapter six. Here attention is drawn to the contribution the financial instruments of capital accounting systems, asset registers and valuation methodologies make to SUD.

Having bridged the gap between these two disciplines, the text develops the connection by providing a framework for analysing SUD and a directory of the environmental assessment methods currently available to appraise land and buildings. Here the language, vocabulary and terms of reference linking both fields of study are introduced to highlight the relationship developing between property management and environmental science. The inter-disciplinary nature of the relationship is examined under the sub-heading of 'valuation and investment appraisal'. Here the inter-disciplinary nature of the development is highlighted in terms of the impact discounting, obsolescence and depreciation have upon the sustainability of the land and buildings making up the urban environment. How, in particular, the discounting mechanism provides a technique of analysis for evaluating the sustainability of urban development.

Landmark developments

The examinations highlight the degree of change property management has recently been subject to. Looked at together, there can be little doubt the changes highlighted in the examination are significant and mark major developments in the field of property management. What-is-more, as landmark developments, the changes can also be seen as representative of the on-going commitment by academics, middle managers, directors and chief executives alike, to make property management more progressive, able in that sense to link with other fields of study which it is connected to. All the examinations that appear in the text are, to a large degree, a product of the progressive agenda which is currently developing and commitment to strengthen the connection property management has with environmental science.

Chapter 2

Property Management

Introduction

This chapter examines the development of property management in terms of the VFM test: land audits; property reviews and transition towards the 3Es. It goes on to look at the consensus emerging over the VFM test and questions the transition to the 3Es has raised about the development of property management. Investigating the 'all-pervasive' marketisation of property management, the examination draws attention to the technical and economic basis of the development. Here attention is drawn to the high-tec, economic cum cultural paradigm of an information rich, communicative form of property management and the place it takes in the re-organisation and reform of services provided under the emerging structures of post-Fordism and neo-Schumpeterian workfare state. The paper draws the investigation to a close by providing some 'sign-posts' in the development of property management.

The VFM test

In the late 1970s it had become generally accepted there was a real need to make large organisations more accountable and subject to a greater degree of audit. With audit came the term 'value for money', what Butt and Palmer (1985) refer to as 'a wide and ambiguous term', but one that, nevertheless, goes a long way to establishing the principle of economy and the use of money as the measure of value attributable to expenditures on goods and services. With the concept of audit and principle of economy came the idea of 'managing better with less', being 'lean, mean, enterprising and competitive'. Based on this managers started to ask the following:

- what accounting procedures are in place;
- how is expenditure audited;
- how could expenditure be made more economic;
- how can the auditing of expenditure be made use of to review the performance of goods and service provision.

In response to this managers started to question whether expenditure met the value for money test. Whether, that is: the accounting and auditing provisions in place are economic and how reviews of expenditure can be carried out to test this. As a consequence, a VFM methodology began to develop. It should be noted that the methodology in question has a relatively simple and straightforward philosophy. In its most simplistic form it can be represented as:

- the definition of the objectives for the test;
- the detailing of the accounting procedures underlying the provision of goods and services;
- the auditing of expenditures;
- a review of performance.

As a set of inter-related activities, the methodology appears quite straightforward. At this level of representation is can be seen as generic, applicable to any situation where accounts are needed and expenditure requires to be audited.

Grounded, as it is in the principle of economy, it is perhaps possible to generalise the objective of the test as value adding - be it in terms of income producing, or cost-saving measures. Working within this objective, the test transforms into a management exercise: one that details the accounting procedures for the provision of the goods and services in question; goes on to audit and on further to establish whether such expenditures can be made more economic through a review of performance. It is perhaps this simple and rather straightforward representation of the VFM test that makes it an attractive management exercise. It should perhaps also be noted that the exercise is not one which is limited to the review of performance, because the information generated from the test, its audit and review, can and often is drawn upon to form the basis of not only a rationalisation, but a thorough and often rigorous re-organisation of the management process underlying the provision of goods and services.

In taking this form, the audit and review issues are represented by the Society of Local Authority Chief Executives (SOLAS, 1986) enquiry into the matter and the Local Authority Valuer's Association (LAVA, 1989) examination of how to manage such exercises. In chronological terms it is a development that is perhaps best marked by Britton, Connellan and Crofts' (1989) representation of such audits and reviews as a form of rationalisation.

Land audits and property reviews

According to Britton, Connellan and Crofts (1989) a land audit or property review, is a process by which systematic attention is given to each interest in landed property by a team of qualified people working to a close brief. Here, the audit and review in question are seen to represent an essential first step towards attaining good management.

In the context of the exercise, 'good management' is defined in terms of the initiatives - in this instance the audit and review - that not only allows the measurement of land and property in terms of 'monetary value', but which also leads to the 'minimum' amount of expenditure on the management of related goods and services. To achieve this Britton, Connellan and Crofts (1989) propose the following. Firstly, the audit and review must be supported by both the professional officers, directors and executives of the corporation in question. In order to achieve this, they propose it is necessary to 'sell' the idea to those within the organisation whom it will affect and in this connection it is important to state from the outset, how the financial proceeds of the exercise are to be distributed within the corporation. Secondly, it must systematically cover all the organisation's landed property, regardless of tenure and use. Thirdly, it should cross all boundaries (geographical and departmental) because land audits and reviews are a corporate activity. Fourthly, the first land audit and review should be planned as a single project with a defined time span which should be as short as possible. If this means that it requires additional resources, these should be costed and provided for in the project, because if the exercise takes too long, the beneficial effects of the audit and review will be diluted. As a rule of thumb, it is suggested a small portfolio of holdings should be audited within twelve months and a medium-sized holding should be reviewed in three years. It is also proposed that the largest portfolios should be audited within the span of a typical rent review period which is five years.

As they go on to point out: one of the main functions of the land audit and property review should be to establish suitable performance indicators for each property interest and to set up systems for the continuous monitoring of performance according to those indicators. The suggested measures of performance are:

- net capital receipts from disposals;
- increases in receipts from income-producing landed property (for example: investment property);
- the reduction in landed property used by the organisaiton;
- the reduction in running costs;
- the ratio of all receipts and savings to the cost of the audit and review.

From this it is evident that land audits and property reviews centre upon the generation of capital receipts from income producing land and property. As such it is an exercise that is geared towards solving the problem of the static estate in organisations, the subsequent mis-match, under-use and relatively high level of vacancy, by the disposal of land and property the audit and review declares surplus to requirements. While the exercise reduces the amount of land and property made use of by the disposal of poorly performing assets and benefits from the consequent improvement such a form of rationalisation brings about, the problem of running cost control appears to take a low priority in the overall scheme of things. This is to some degree borne out by the fact questions about running cost control only appear towards the bottom of the list. It is perhaps this switch of concern from the generation of capital receipts via the said audits and reviews, to the reduction of running costs, that marks the transition from rationalisation to re-organisation. While it is appreciated the distinctions drawn here between VFM, land audits, property reviews, rationalisations and re-organisation are subtle, they are nonetheless critical for the reason they signify that:

- in responding to the VFM test, the management of property has been augmented by initiatives in land audit geared towards the review of property and assessment of whether land and property held by an organisation meets their requirements, if there is a mis-match, under use of assets, or high level of vacancy;
- in placing a monetary value on the holdings the opportunity cost of land and property ownership is established, along with the price of holding assets that are unsuitable, partially used or vacant;
- the high cost of holding inappropriate assets tends to illustrate the price of owing such resources is too high and uneconomic in real terms, a situation which tends to force a redistribution of land and property through realisation and disposal;
- the outcome of such an exercise represents a form of rationalisation and drive towards economy in the allocation of assets;
- in seeking to consolidate the gains realised from such a form of rationalisation, attention has now begun to switch from the audit and review of holdings as a stock of land and property, towards the stream of expenditure on the goods and services required to manage the assets in question;
- this focuses attention on the static estate (the so-called mis-match, under-use of assets and question of vacant property) and problem of running cost control - the need for an audit and review of the growing expenditures on the stock and flow of goods and services paid out to cover the cost of managing property;
- following this, a number of additional initiatives have surfaced which looked at together represent a deep and thorough re-organisation of property management.

It is evident that in taking this form, the movement towards the 3Es represents a growing interest in the economics the audit, review, rationalisation and subsequent process of re-organisation forming part of the drive towards a greater degree of efficiency and effectiveness from the management of property.

Towards the 3Es

As already pointed out, Britton, Connellan and Crofts (1989) define good management in terms of: measuring the value of property in monetary terms and employing the minimum amount of expenditure on its management. Having defined 'good' management in such a way, they go on to suggest such a form of property management: deserves the adjectives, 'economic', 'efficient' and 'effective', as the landed property will be maintained on a business-like footing, producing sufficient benefit (performance of duties and attainment of objectives) at minimum possible cost. While economic, the authors also go on to suggest, based on a 'business-like' footing, such a form of management will be efficient because it produces the desired effect (provision of landed property to enable the organisation to perform its duties and attain its objectives) with the minimum possible input of resources. In addition, they also go on to suggest that it will be effective because this will have the desired effect of providing landed property which enables the corporation in question to perform its duties and attain set objectives. As they go on to point out: unfortunately it is not common to find such a form of property management, because in the past the management of property has been subject to two major problems - what they refer to as:

- the static estate and;
- problem of running cost control.

The term 'static estate' is perhaps a little confusing in the sense it introduces another variable into the equation. What-is-more, it begs the question about the exact nature of the relationship between the estate and landed property: something that also raises a question about the relationship between land and property and why the management focus is not on the former but the latter. As such it is a matter that requires clarification. The term estate is made use of by Britton, Connellan and Crofts (1989) because over the past one hundred years it is the estate which has formed the subject of interest from the academic point of view and it is only over the post-war period that such studies have drawn a distinction between the estate as an ownership of land and other forms of property in terms of fixed and circulating capital - the outcome of this being the appearance of terms such as landed estate or landed property as attempts to highlight the fixed nature of such assets as combinations of land and capital. Again in chronological terms, it ought to be recognised that the term estate is often drawn upon where the structure of tenure relates to the landlord's interest i.e. in the ownership of land, the opposite situation being the case where the term property is made use of due to the fact it tends to transcend the interest of the landlord and include the tenant's occupational interest i.e. in the land and capital forming the fixed asset required for operational purposes.

In contrast to the partial, land-based interest of the estate, the term property tends to suggest a more comprehensive representation of the material (land and buildings as forms of fixed capital assets) forming the subject of management. It is this partial, land-based interest that Britton, Connellan and Crofts (1989) evoke in using the term static estate. Here the term static is drawn upon to characterise how such an interest can perhaps best be described and it is from this that we get a number of definitions geared towards the characterisation of the estate in comparison to property management (see Table 2.1).

Table 2.1   Characterisation of Estate and Property Management

Management	Estate	Property
	Static	Dynamic
	Inert	Active
	Reactive	Pro-Active
	Unresponsive	Responsive
	Partial	Comprehensive

The authors in question suggest that such an unfortunate characterisation stems, to a large degree, from the lack of consensus in academic circles as to the purpose of the estate and the exact nature of its relationship to property management and while no clear conclusion is drawn in their discussions on the matter, it is evident there is a tendency to associate estate management with the legal and social structure underlying the division of tenure into a landlord and tenant relation, rather than and as opposed to the corporate, financial and commercial dimensions of property management. The problem with leaving the subject at the legal and social level of analysis is seen to lie in the tendency it has to put the estate in what is referred to as in a state of 'hypostatis'. In a state, that is, where the estate becomes inert to the developments in its environment and unresponsive to the underlying pressure the market places upon it to change. As a consequence, management under this set of circumstances is seen to be reactive to the demands the market places upon it and tactical in any measures it takes to tackle problems in the legal and social structure of tenure.

In contrast to this and in being seen to take on a more comprehensive form, property management, rather than seeing such pressures as external, attempts to embody such developments and use the dynamics of the market place to become pro-active and responsive to demands for change. The value of having such qualities is seen to lie in the fact that together they allow property management to transcend the static estate forming the legal and social structure of tenure and work with the market to develop a corporate, financial and commercial strategy able to tackle the pressing problem of running cost control. For Britton, Connellan and Crofts (1989) such qualities are seen to be critical because without them it would not be possible to transcend the limitations of the legal and social structure of tenure underlying (and giving rise to) the static estate, or develop the corporate, financial instruments or commercial standards required to achieve this. As critical components in the movement towards the 3Es in property management, such qualities are seen to be indispensable, because without them there would not be a corporate, financial or commercial strategy capable of solving the problem of running cost control.

In assessing the response to the call for the development of a strategic approach to property management, the authors point out that professional experts in this field see the options available to them in the following terms:

• do nothing;

- further encourage the breakdown of 'departmentalism';
- set up new organisational structures to assist the breakdown of departmentalism;
- adopt the principle of pro-active management of property as a dynamic resource;
- prepare a corporate statement on property management;
- create a central, preferably computer-based information system for the management of property;
- adopt appropriate accounting procedures;
- audit and review property holdings;
- introduce asset rents as a capital charge for the use of property;
- set up property trading accounts.

If we discount the 'do nothing' option, the list highlights the need to set up new organisational structures capable of breaking down departmentalism, bringing about pro-active management and having the ability to see property as ˊ dynamic resource. This is a situation the authors see as being brought about by a modernisation of property management along the lines of proper registration, audits, review and valuation for the calculation of asset rents and capital charges - not to mention commercial trading of assets. In taking this form, it is evident the discussion has much in common with the initiatives underlying VFM in terms of a search for accountability through audit, review and drive towards economy. Perhaps the critical point of difference in this instance, however, lies in the less partial and more comprehensive nature of the audit and review. The fact, that is, the exercise is not limited to a audit and review of holdings i.e. stocks, but takes on a form which includes the flow of services. In other words: takes on the form of an exercise that searches for not just economy in the management of the standing stock but economy, efficiency and effectiveness in both the income payments and cost outgoings which underlie the stock of holdings and flow of services. Perhaps of even greater significance is the fact that they see this as something which requires proper registration, audit, review and valuation. If, that is, the transition from VFM to the 3Es is to develop a strategy which is better equipped to manage property.

Strategic management

The discussion of what is referred to as, 'strategic management' seeks to examine what the Institute of Directors (IOD, 1991) refer to as: 'the coming of age for property management; the development of property as a matter of strategic concern to management at the 'boardroom' level of chief executives and directorates'. How this has taken place is illustrated in Figure 2.1.

Figure 2.1 illustrates the relationship between the VFM test and movement towards the 3Es. As such the figure can be read as a set of relationships which for the purpose of explanation break down into three inter-related columns. Read vertically (from bottom to top) the first column illustrates the following:

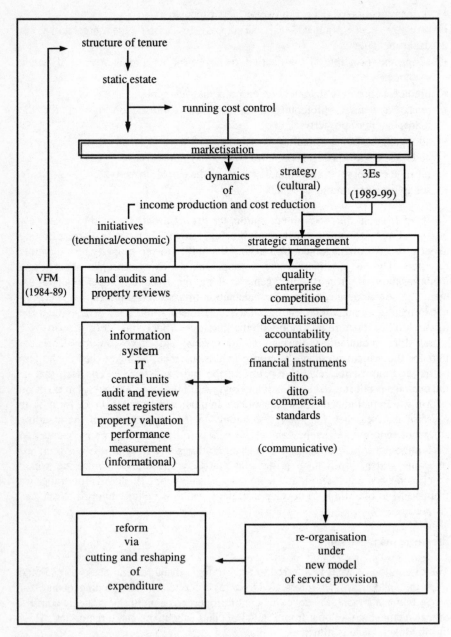

Figure 2.1   Towards Strategic Management

- the VFM test as providing the basis to resolve the issues surrounding the breakdown of the landlord-tenant structure of tenure and subsequent view of property holdings as a static estate i.e. stock of goods not requiring any management expertise - the situation which in this instance has given rise to the problem of running cost control;
- such problems have led to the marketisation of property and the search by management for the 'dynamics of income production' from land audits and property reviews. Land audits and property reviews whose underlying technical and economic qualities are seen as value adding initiatives in terms of the income they produce. Audits and reviews whose income producing qualities are also seen to be enterprising in the way they expose the stock of property to the workings of competitive environments;
- it is at this point property management develops along the lines of additional initiatives, or in terms of both the income producing and cost reduction measures of strategic management;
- this in turn leads to the search for additional initiatives, whereby attention turns to the information systems and IT needed to support land audits and property reviews;
- the way audit and reviews inform decisions taken by the central property units about the registration of assets and valuation of property undertaken for performance measurement purposes;
- how the other route to the marketisation of property management is back through the dynamics of income production, cost reduction and culture of strategy 'on route' to the 3Es. That is through further developments in the quality, enterprise and competitiveness of property management;
- how, once again, this development turns towards the information systems and IT required to decentre decision making and make the management of property accountable as a corporate resource;
- how this set of developments serve to make the management of property (under the aforementioned pro-quality, enterprise-minded, competitive and decentred market regime) more accountable. More accountable in the sense that the strategic management of property subjects central units to a process of corporatisation (across- departmental and ongoing audit and reviews) which in turn requires (in addition to the registers, valuations and measurement of performance forming the informational basis of property management) the development of financial instruments and commercial standards. Financial instruments and commercial standards whose structure of communication leads to the form of cost control, re-organisation and reform set out in the illustration. The re-organisation that develops a new model of service provision and reform which in turn leads to a control of costs via a cutting and reshaping of expenditure.

The underlying developments

Figure 2.3 identifies the developments underlying the transition from estate to property management over the post-war era. As can also be seen, it characterises the problem property management has faced over the period in question as that of the 'static estate'. The static estate and the problems of running cost control, vacant, or under-used premises and mis-match of the demands placed on the management of property relative to supply. It also illustrates that since 1983/84, property management has sought to become pro-active in the management of holdings and develop a number of initiatives which provide a solution to the problems of the static estate. The solution in question appears in the next heading under the title of 'towards a strategic response'. Hence what the diagram draws attention to is the initiatives forming the content of strategies A, B and C listed towards the right-hand side of the illustration.

The initiatives are those responses which attempt to treat property as a dynamic resource, requiring pro-active management. They include: for example; the adoption of VFM as standards of accountability, land audits, property reviews, surveys, measurements and appraisals, the application of information technology, formation of organisational structures and other such measures geared towards the improvement of property management. Strategies A, B and C relate to the strategic responses taken to try and incorporate such standards into the management of property. Here the emphasis is not so much to do with the type of initiative and all its particular requirements (manpower, technical expertise, organisational skills, expenditure, etc) but on where it fits into the overall structure of property management. Where, if you like, VFM, accountability, audit, review, surveys, measurement and appraisals fit into a strategy towards the 3Es. As such, the question is not about what technical merits the initiative offers, but the cost of it and what value it will add to the management of property defined in economic, efficient and effective terms.

In this instance, Strategy A is that part of the response put forward by Britton, Connellan and Crofts (1989) in their examination of property management in the public sector, Strategy B is Gibson, Gibson and Watt's (1989) examination of operational property asset management in the independent sector and Avis, Crosby, French and Gibson's (1993) study of property management in terms of performance monitoring. Hence, and as can be seen, the strategic response is one that examines the management of property in terms of operational and investment assets. Strategy C represents Avis and Gibson's (1995) more recent exploration of what they term real estate resource management. The heading Strategies 2 draws attention to the content of strategies A, B and C. In that sense, the strategies which have developed towards the corporatisation of property, development of financial instruments and commercial standards, put forward to solve the problem of running cost control (also, see Weatherhead, 1997).

Post-war	1983/84	1986	1989	1993	1995
problem	**solution**	**towards a strategic response**			
static estate	dynamics	initiatives	strategies 1		
			A	B	C
running cost control vacant or under-used premises and mis-match of property	towards the pro-active management of property holdings	value for money, accountability, land audit, property review, surveying, measurement and appraisal, application of IT central units, income and cost related issues, current cost accounting, asset rents and capital charges as forms of income, consideration of outgoing payments	economic, efficient and effective management	management of operational property assets and performance monitoring of operational and investment property	real estate resource management
			strategies 2		
			corporatisation financial instruments commercial standards		
Estate	**Property Management**				

Figure 2.2 Developments Underlying the Transition

The emerging consensus

The aforementioned reference to strategies A, B and C, tends to suggest there is some form of consensus emerging over the development of property management. To some extent this is true. How true is perhaps the question that ought to be asked. Why? Because the consensus in question tends to be limited to the 'broad picture', not the detail of the development! This of course, begs the supplementary question, what is the emerging consensus? In brief terms, it is the thesis that VFM, land audits and property reviews, represent a rationalisation of property management aimed at bringing the standards of services in the public sector into line with those of the private. The idea in particular that in becoming quality-minded, enterprising and competitive, property management in local authorities - the public sector in general for that matter - is compatible, if not equivalent, to that in the private. Compatible in the sense property management in the public sector is based upon the same set of values as those in the private: values such as competition, enterprise and the like and belief that the moneterisation of them in terms of pricing, cost calculations and income projections, will lead to greater economy, efficiency and effectiveness - all of which, it ought to be added, is seen to be a 'good' thing because it is understood to be in the public interest.

As already pointed out, this 'privatisation thesis' can be seen to represent the emerging consensus. If we look at the main components of property management, the consensus on the matter can be seen to break down into disagreements over the detail. The main components of property management in local authorities relate to:

- the purpose of local authorities under the transition;
- central property units;
- asset registers;
- property valuation;
- performance measurement.

Regarding the first question, few academics or professional experts appear to directly support the idea of privatisation and seek instead to emphasise the merits of VFM and the 3Es as a form of review and rationalisation. One that is not only seen to re-organise the services the property management division of a local authority can provide in adopting such measures, but also reform the quality of the product on offer (see Britton, Connellan and Crofts, 1989; French, 1994). On the question of central property units, again there appears to be no objection to the principle of centralising the organisation of command and control functions in the property management divisions of local authorities and introducing innovative landlord and tenant-type structures to divide the management of property in such authorities along strategic and routine day-to-day lines. Again, if the said management division is to become the custodian or steward of property held by a local authority, there is no objection to the register acting as an inventory of holdings. Perhaps of greater significance are the questions that have recently been raised over:

- the technical basis, classes and categories of asset valuations;
- the lack of methodological advice;
- confusion over the distinction between costs in use and exchange;
- the distinctive nature of the cost and income approaches to the valuation of property;
- the reduction of property valuation to a financial analysis of annuities, notional interest and depreciation in current cost accounting, capital charging and asset rents;
- the use of such information as a basis to 'evaluate' the stock of assets, streams of services and subsequent rationalisation of holdings;
- the tendency for financial instruments of this type to discriminate - in terms of performance measurement - against cost-based holdings and favour income-producing property.

As can be seen, the questions arise out of the uncertainty and risk, or novelty of the exercise and can be read as a request for further clarification in terms of guidelines, recommended procedures etc. This is particularly noticeable with the first three questions. The subsequent questions are a little more difficult to deal with because they relate to confusion over the technical basis of property valuations that is subsequently compounded due to resulting methodological problems. It is the question of method that has attracted most attention to date. It is seen to represent a problem of such a magnitude that Young (1994) goes so far as to ask why such an exercise has been embarked upon.

Young (1994) appears to be of the mind that the uncertainties and confusion surrounding the development of property management in local authorities are of such a magnitude they seriously bring into question the logic of the whole exercise. This is because for Young (1994), the introduction of neo-liberal principles about the virtues of competition, enterprise and a greater degree of quantification in the allocation of resources, appears to have little significance, neither does the fact such instruments allow decisions about the management of property to reflect the opportunity cost (scarcity and transfer earnings) of income payments, outgoings, capital and interest. If this can be taken to represent the underlying purpose of the exercise, i.e. the introduction of market competition and enterprise in the moneterisation of values (vis-à-vis quantification), then the question which follows is - how is it to be done? How, in other words, is it possible to circumvent the questions raised about the transition to the 3Es in the development of property management. If we are to answer this, we have first of all to recognise it is not an easy undertaking because there are no immediate solutions to the problems in question. Moreover, we have to recognise the problems lie with the theory of property valuation, rather than the technology and methodologies of its management.

The theory of property valuation

At present, the theory of property valuation is divided along the pro-income line of Baum and Mackmin (1989), Brown (1991), Baum and Crosby (1996) and that of cost (see, Britton, Connellan and Crofts, 1989). The former has its origins in the Fisher inspired thesis of 'income over cost' as a rate of return, while the latter shares Marshall's concern over opportunity cost, scarcity and transfer earnings in the distribution of income as a reward for the 'productivity of capital'. Another initial distinction lies in the tendency for the advocates of the neo-Austrian school of economic thought to adopt a classical notion of liberty under the law of exchange, trade and commerce. The latter, like the Cambridge School in general, is sceptical about the theory of an equilibrium under perfect competition and chose instead to focus attention on the imperfect nature of markets as allocative mechanisms. The imperfect nature and inability of the market to provide public, community or merit goods and services and subsequent need for legal and social reforms if the mechanism is to be economic, efficient and equitable (see, Blaug 1992). The distinction drawn between the two schools of thought, however, is significant because the politics of the modern welfare state tends to divide the valuation of property along progressive and conservative lines of the Cambridge and Austrian Schools respectively.

Progressive and conservative divisions

Under the progressive legal and social reforms of the modern welfare state, the government is required to follow Keynesian doctrine on employment, money and interest so as to manage economic growth through fiscal means. The fiscal means required to fund public expenditure, supplement the market with statutory instruments allowing for the regulation of property rights, planning of development, control of land use and provision of public, community, merit goods and services - be it in the direct or subsidised form. The fiscal means - taxation in particular - regulation, planning, control and provision of goods and services - it should be noted - also required to re-distribute income in the aim of producing a level of demand sufficient to generate full employment, rising standards of living, the Pareto-optima efficiency criteria and equity condition of Rawlsian social justice. The said aims, criteria and conditions that legitimates the management of economic growth, fiscal means, statutory powers and planning instruments underlying the redistribution of income, legal and social reforms of the modern welfare state.

It is a form of management the conservative elements of the neo-Austrian school object to. This is because the Keynesian doctrine of demand management is seen to undermine liberty and freedom and in so doing, replacing the law of consumer sovereignty governing economic growth, employment, money and interest, with the politics of administration. An administrative form of reason seen by the Austrian School to represent the antithesis of competition and enterprise, due to the 'fact' that its fiscal means for funding public expenditure not only replaces the freedom of the market with regulation, planning and control, but perhaps more significantly redistributes income (via the various legal and social reforms of the welfare state) in a way which leads to the growth of bureaucracies whose 'extra-market' instruments, turns the demand management of Keynesian doctrine into the cost-push inflation of employment, money and interest. This is a situation that, for them - and many others for that matter - is seen to mark the end of the pro-growth model of the redistributive welfare state, onset of stagflation, decline in employment and rise in the monetary and interest charges, which makes public expenditure on legal and social reform too costly a measure. Not only in the sense of the tax burden required to fund any such measures, but also due to the cost (relative to income) of supplying labour, capital and land in the production of goods and services. Costs seen to be so high as to make the employment of labour, capital and land in the production of goods and services uneconomic and so challenge the pro-growth redistributive logic of legal and social reform under the welfare state.

Legitimation crisis

It is the situation Habermas (1976) refers to as the 'legitimation crisis' of the welfare state. The situation whereby the Keynesian doctrine of demand management results in costs of production which are uneconomic and inefficient in terms of the distribution of income its legal and social reforms produce for employment and the standard of living. For in its advanced stage of development, the welfare state is unable to meet either of these aims, or draw upon sufficient mass support to legitimate any new fiscal measures. Indeed, it is a situation that is seen to expose what Offe (1984) describes as the contradictions of the welfare state and shift to a more conservative administration. One that substitutes 'cost-push' for 'demand pull', monetarist for Keynesian doctrine and reinstates the law of consumer sovereignty in the shift from 'state to market' via privatisation - the so-called deregulation, opening up and liberalisation of property rights in accordance with market competition and enterprise.

It is a situation Bell (1973) refers to as 'post-industrialisation' and others for example, Giddens (1990), Lash and Urry (1987,93) and Jessop (1993) term the crisis of Fordist mass production under the Keynesian welfare state. The crisis Lash and Urry (1987, 93) and Jessop (1993) refer to not only in legal and social, but economic terms and see as representing the transition to post-Fordism and the neo-Schumpeterian workfare state (see Jessop, 1993 in particular). The transition that incorporates and oversees the dismantling of the welfare state, disengagement of government from the management of economic growth, deregulation of markets, fostering of competition and enterprise, removal of fiscal measures, loosening of planning and development, redistribution of the tax burden, control of money supply and interest rates, via tight public expenditure.

Whether this shift has taken place under Thatcher or Reagan, the new discursive reality traversing the state can be described as a pervasive 'manageralisation' discourse, which aims to make marketisation the driving force of an enterprising and competitively successful public sector. It is clearly linked to the proliferation of managerial panaceas issuing from the USA during the 1980's, claiming to offer genuinely novel 'business' solutions to the problems accumulating from the need to adapt organisationally to rapidly changing and confusing market conditions.

The new manageralism and market reasoning

The most profound accomplishment of this discourse may not be that it literally rolls back the state in order to release the full blast of market forces but, rather, that it inserts a new managerialism and market reasoning into the state and state-related agencies of the public sector, in effect calling upon organisations that are not themselves private businesses to think and function as though they were. The effect of these powerful and normalising discourses is to make it virtually impossible to think outside of them. This may be illustrated by a book which, in the early 1990s became a major codification for new managerialist theory and practice in the public sector on both sides of the Atlantic, Osborne and Gaebler's (1992) *Reinventing Government*. Drawing on the ideas of management gurus such as Drucker and Peters, their managerial principles are drawn from practical experiments conducted by US city governments in response to the 'tax revolts' of the late 1970s and more broadly, the structural transformations brought about by the transition to post-Fordism. Under tight budgetary constraints and faced with radically transformed economic circumstances, it is proposed that governments have to become much more 'enterprising' then they had been during the 'bureaucratic-industrial' era. The 'principles' of the theory Osborne and Gaebler (1992: 19-20) put forward for good management are as follows:

> Most entrepreneurial governments promote competition between service providers. They empower citizens by pushing control out of the bureaucracy, into the community. They measure the performance of their agencies, focusing not on inputs but on outcomes. They are driven by their goals - their missions - not by their rules and regulations. They redefine their clients as customers and offer them choices - between schools, between training programs, between housing options. They prevent problems before they emerge, rather than simply offering services afterwards. They put their energies into earning money, not simply spending it. They decentralise authority, embracing participatory management. They prefer market mechanisms. And they focus not simply on providing public services, but on catalysing all sectors - public, private and voluntary - into action to solve their community's problems.

Although Osborne and Gaebler (1992) deny asking for government to be 'run like a business', their ideas undoubtedly originate from the ideas about corporatisation being adopted by city governments and the local authorities they represent.

The discursive moment in the UK and USA

It is a 'discursive moment' that McGuigan (1996) describes as a shift towards the philosophy of 'VFM' and the '3Es' under post-Fordism and the movement towards a neo-Schumptereian workfare state, characterised by an increasingly pervasive market reasoning and managerialist rhetoric from the late 1970s and to the present and foreseeable future. The UK examples of this have already been set out and appear in the form of Butt and Palmer (1985); Britton, Connellan and Crofts (1989); Avis, Gibson and Watts (1989) and Weatherhead's (1997) research. The US position has not yet been set out and while influential in the research of Avis, Gibson and Watt (1989); Avis and Gibson (1995) and Weatherhead (1997) is worth examining for the fact its case studies include Ford's own response to the crisis in question. The research in question includes that of Veale (1988), Joroff, Lovargand, Lambert and Franklin (1993). The standard textbook representation is provided by Brown and Arnold (1993).

In the case of the USA, the emphasis is not so much on the transition from estate to property management, as corporate real estate and initiatives making up what is termed the 'strategic management of the fifth resource'. As Joroff, Lovargand, Lambert and Franklin (1993) point out, in the early 1980s corporate managers, consultants and researchers set to work in transforming four major resources - capital, manpower, technology and information. Until now, however, real estate has not figured in this transformation. What they suggest is that real estate represents the corporation's last under-managed resource. These conclusions are drawn from surveys undertaken in 1981 and 87 respectively. Now it is argued, leaders in the field of corporate real estate recognise this under-development of the subject and are participating in the search for a strategic management of the fifth resource. The reasons put forward for this are as follows:

- mergers;
- outsourcing;
- divesture;
- downsizing.

Taken together these changes are seen to signal a deep and thorough economic re-organisation. An economic re-organisation so deep and thorough, it is argued that if corporations are to remain profitable, they must change from the mass production of the past and become more competitive - through cost cutting, rationalisations (mergers, divestiture, downsizing, outsourcing) - and enterprising in 'tailoring' appropriate responses to the developments in question.

Here the 'tailoring' of the appropriate response is taken to represent the development of corporate real estate management in general and the corporate management of real estate as the fifth strategic resource in particular. In essence, the research identifies two dimensions to the development; the first being the design and organisation of real estate units; the second being the financial management of the resource as a form of corporate strategy. Both these dimensions are then underpinned by an examination of how IT automates real estate and acts as both the informational and communicative structure for its corporate management. The research identifies five stages to the evolutionary development of corporate real estate units, they are as follows:

- taskmaster - supplies the corporation's need for physical space as requested;
- controller - satisfies senior management's need to better understand and minimise real estate costs;
- dealmaker - solves real estate problems in ways that create financial value for the business units;
- intrapreneur - operates like an internal real estate company, proposing real estate alternatives to the business units that match those of the firm's competitors;
- strategist - anticipates business trends, monitors and measures their impacts; contributes to the value of the corporation as a whole by focusing on the company's mission rather than focusing only on real estate.

Putting these tasks into the evolutionary development of corporate real estate management, Joroff, Lovargand, Lambert and Franklin (1993) represent the engineering approach of the 'taskmaster' as the traditional role of the real estate manager - the skills and expertise that correspond to the 'static estate' in the UK example. The 'cost minimiser / controller' is also taken to represent the response of real estate managers to decline. It is the 'deal-maker' stage that is taken to represent the start up of real estate corporate management and its subsequent growth and maturity under the 'intrapreneur' and 'strategist' stages. As illustrated in Table 2.3, it is at this 'deal-maker' stage that VFM and the 3Es appear in the transition from the traditional to contemporary situation and where real estate becomes the corporate management of the fifth strategic resource. Table 2.3 also introduces the financial dimension to corporate estate management in the form of the fourth and fifth columns relating to both capital costs and pricing.

Learning from Ford's re-engineering

While the research by Joroff, Lovargand, Lambert and Franklin (1993) is based on case-studies drawn from Kodak, IBM, Hewlett Packard, Kraft and Sun Microsystems - effecttively from corporations across the whole industrial structure - Ford is put forward to exemplify how, under this organisation's corporate management, real estate becomes the fifth strategic resource. This is illustrated by the following quote:

> Ford Motor Land Development Corp. is an unusual kind of real estate organisation. Created in 1970 to develop some 2,300 acres of land in Dearborn, Mich., the unit spent the first 17 years of its life as a real estate developer operating with the benefit of its alliance with a major tenant, Ford Motor Company.
>
> [Task master / Controller]

In 1987 it began to accept responsibility for corporate real estate services for Ford Motor Co on a worldwide basis and for the development of dealership properties. The gradual transformation from real estate developer to real estate services group was recently completed by its acceptance of European real estate operations and worldwide construction responsibility. These two steps completed the merger of the development group with Ford's internal real estate services.

[Deal Maker]

Ford Land uses its development background to educate its business units on the real value of space. Bob Jackson, president and COO of Ford Land, says that some business units have begun to examine their occupancies and land holdings and ask Ford Land whether they can capture hidden value from their real estate, having seen the results in other areas of the company.

[Intrapreneur]

Ford Land is also sensitive to the issues raised at the level of the Intrapreneur. Ford's internal training centre long occupied a 1929 school building. Due to substantial increases in demand for training from Ford and supplier companies, the training unit sought new space. A greenfield development site was identified and planning was well underway when it became clear that a Ford-operated banquet facility posed an attractive alternative to new construction. In recent years alternative facilities opened in the area, including hotels and a private club. By deciding to shut down a profitable but redundant operation, the banquet facility, Ford Land demonstrates the value of accumulating ever more sophisticated real estate strategies.

[Strategist]

They tripled the training centre capacity at only a 30 per cent increase in cost, and made the kind of decision that capital markets have come to expect more frequently. Ford had a profitable operation in the banquet facility but the returns to that capital will be substantially higher in the alternative use. This kind of efficiency should get rewarded in the share pricing mechanism.

Ford's decision shows a portfolio approach to asset management. By looking at assets in combination, the team at Ford saw that conversion of the banquet facility to a training centre would have at least two positive synergistic effects. First, the hotel occupancy in the immediate vicinity would be enhanced, and second, the kitchen facilities at the adjacent club could be used to service the training centre, putting those resources to more efficient use. While using a portfolio approach and satisfying capital market demands, Ford also serviced the goal of cost minimisation.

It is this 'evolutionary shift', or re-engineering of Taylor's *Scientific Management* that is of interest to Lash and Urry (1987, 94) and Urry (1995) in their examination of the shift towards much more 'reflexive' systems of producer services in the USA, Germany and Japan. Here attention is drawn to the high design, discursive skills and expertise (theoretical rather than practical knowledge) underlying the IT systems of the less vertical (hierarchical) more horizontal (flatter) communicative structures for the development of such 'small batch' (tailored) producer services. Producer services, whose response to the economic re-organisation has been to transcend both the static estate and need for cost-control by becoming more competitive and enterprising in developing the cultural dimension to corporate management. The cultural dimension to corporate management, which in adopting the financial instruments and IT of horizontal, flatter communicative structures, is forced to face the risk and uncertainties that characterise the market.

Table 2.2   Development of Corporate Real Estate

Initiatives/ Strategies	Decision Criteria	Products	Capital Cost	Pricing	Evolutionary Stage
Engineering Approach (Taskmaster)	Business unit wants	Taj Mahals and palaces *RE costs out of control*	Absorbed as corporate costs	Accounting for cost	Tradition (Static Estate)
Cost Minimisation (Controller)	Traditional control standards	Low cost palaces *Cost savings but no competitive standards*	Business units pay depreciation	Cost Accounting	Decline (Cost Control)
Market Cost and Usage Standards (Dealmaker)	Market economics drive RE decisions	Spec building quality *Lower costs and competitive standards*	Business units may pay opportunity cost of capital	Value Adding	Start up (Value for Money)
Market Design Approach (Intrapreneur)	RE unit makes decisions like a RE company	Spec building design standards leveraging needs with the market *Savings and profits*	Business units pay market rent	Real estate market pricing	Growth (Economy)
Business Strategy Approach (Strategist)	Business strategy drives R E decisions	Innovative buildings and location strategies *Savings, profits and strategic advantage*	Business units must justify market rents	Capital market pricing	Maturity (Efficient and Effective Management of a Portfolio)

As such, and as Lash and Urry (1987,94) and Urry (1995) point out, the developments in question are not just a response to economic re-organisation, but like McGuigan (1996) and Webster (1997) suggest, in promoting quality rather than quantity, enterprise and competition are also cultural phenomena and can only be understood as part of the discourse on the new scientific principles of corporate management (the so-called managerialist thesis) under post-Fordism and the neo-Schumpeterian workfare state (Jessop, 1993). Albeit, in this instance, a discourse on its application to corporate management and the development of real estate as the fifth strategic resource.

It is perhaps a little ironic that in the case of corporate real estate management, it should be Ford who provides the 'best' example of a response to the crisis of Fordism under the welfare state and in taking the form it does, also provides a new model of corporate real estate management not only for the private sector, but for city governments as local authorities. The case study also goes a long way to demonstrate just how all pervasive the marketisation is. For as the example illustrates, it provides a new model of corporate real estate not only for the private sector, but the management of city governments as local authorities under the post-Fordist, neo-Schumpeterian workfare state.

Tailoring the UK response

If for the moment, it can be assumed that property may be substituted for real estate, it becomes evident that Gibson's (1986, 1991, 1994 and 1995) research (along with Avis, Gibson and Watts, 1989; Avis and Gibson, 1995) mirrors that currently taking place in the USA and represents an attempt to examine the relationship between IT, the corporate and financial dimensions to the management of property. As such it attempts to redress the imbalance, or asymmetric relationship that has previously existed between initiatives and strategy. In doing so, it centres attention on the role of initiatives in the development of corporate strategy and the financial dimensions of property management.

There can be little doubt that the research undertaken by Gibson, Avis, Gibson and Watts (1995), opens up a number of possibilities for those with a particular interest in the development of property management. It is valuable for the fact the research introduces the technical concerns over the informational basis of IT applications, the communicative structures of corporate strategy and the financial dimensions of property management. The programme of research can perhaps best be seen as a sign-post marking a significant development in the transition from estate to property management. For what it does is switch attention away from the technical and economic concerns over the informational basis of IT applications for asset registers, property valuation, auditing, review and performance measurement (initiatives), to the culture of communication surrounding the corporate strategy and financial dimensions of property management. It is this theme that Weatherhead (1997) also develops in her studies of corporate strategy and finance in IBM, BT, Marks and Spencer, Sainsbury's and Boots.

While significant and marking an important step forward, the research has to be put into context: firstly; there are some obvious difficulties over the 'Anglophonic' use of the terms real estate and property: secondly; the research tends to 'downplay' the technical and economic concerns about initiatives in the informational basis of communicative structures in favour of the cultural question surrounding the corporate strategy and financial instruments required for such purposes: thirdly; as a consequence, the management thesis tends to 'blur' any distinction between values in terms of the technical, economic and cultural composition of either the informational basis, communicative structures, corporate strategy and financial instruments in question: fourthly; all the publications from this school of thought are ambivalent about the relationship between the public and independent sectors.

It is perhaps Hambleton (1990) and Cochrane (1993) who best draw attention to the significance of the new manageralist thesis in the sense that in attempting to 'turn professionals into managers', it produces a set of experts who are unaware, insensitive and poorly educated as to the forms of service provision (also, see Lash and Urry, 1993; Urry, 1995). The fact that structures of provision i.e. the combination of initiatives and strategy can be pro-private and public, central-administrative, bureaucratic, decentralised-market, consumer-orientated, based on uniform, or plural values, elitist or popularist, is something which tends to be missed by advocates of the managerialist thesis. What Hambleton (1990) and Cochrane (1993) draw attention to the effect the corporate strategy and financial instruments have upon the management of service provision and their underlying purpose. Noting the effect of the strategy and instruments is to produce a 'new model of service provision', they propose the underlying purpose of the exercise lies in a 'cutting and reshaping of expenditure'. Reflecting on this matter it is suggested that:

- the cutting and reshaping of expenditure which occurs under the new model of service provision represents a re-organisation of service provision;
- this in turn reforms service provision via:
  - privatisation;
  - an improvement in the responsiveness of managers to consumer demand;
  - an empowerment of the consumer for the purposes of strengthening democracy.

While Hambleton (1990) draws upon Hoggett's (1987, 1989) thesis on the crisis of the long-standing association between Taylorist-type organisations and Fordist-based mass production, the subsequent demise of a strong, centralist welfare-state and shift towards post-Fordism (see Stoker, 1990 and Cochrane, 1993), what is noticeable is the degree to which all three forms of response to the new 'high-tech, economic cum cultural paradigm' of 'information rich communication', focuses upon the question of strategy. That is the technology, economics and culture of the informational basis and communicative structures, which both reorganise and reforms property management by either privatisation, improving the responsiveness to consumer demand, or by the strengthening of democracy (also, see Urry 1995; McGuigan, 1996 and Webster, 1997).

The influence of the first form can be traced back to Peters and Waterman (1982) and Osbourne and Gaebler (1992) in terms of the USA, with Butt and Palmer (1985) providing the UK examples. The emphasis here being on the cultural dimension to the development and in that sense the use of language, theory and method by management in the design and modelling of the corporate strategy and financial instruments required to either privatise, improve responsiveness, or democratise the provision of services.

This is an issue Gibson (1991) reflects on in asking the question of who manages 'operational' property best? Interestingly, after noting the similarities between the independent and public sectors, Gibson (1991) finds the development of the corporate strategies and financial instruments make it difficult to establish whether the 'privatisation' of one sector means it is better at providing VFM and the 3Es better than the other. To date it appears that there is no research within the new managerialist thesis which has attempted to look at the AC reports or activities of CIPFA as a means to improve the responsiveness to consumer needs. While this ethic appears to be that 'embedded' in the earlier research of Britton, Connellan and Crofts (1989), the report in question only serves to document the early stages of the transition from estate to property management and is unable to establish the degree to which corporate strategy and financial instruments have been able to improve the quality of service provision and become more responsive to consumer needs. It is a line of enquiry Deakin (1997a, b) has sought to further by providing particular case-study examples of the response in question. By, in this instance, examining how the technology and economics of a pro-quality, enterprise-minded culture and decentralised market, provide a communicative structure competitive enough to resolve the problem of running cost control.

Model of property management

The model of property management this chapter wishes to represent is set out in Figure 2.3. As can be seen, this model of property management draws upon the previous discussions and represents the subject in terms of:

- the initiatives and strategies that make up the modernisation of property management;
- the informational and communicative structures of property management;
- the re-organisation and reform the said structures have in turn been subject to as part of this development.

Development	
The Static Estate	Running Cost Control
Initiatives	*Strategies*
(Technical) VFM Land Audits Property Reviews Markets Information Systems Central Units Asset Rents under Capital Accounting Contracting (Economics)	The Three Es Quality Enterprise Competitive Decentred Accountable Corporate (Culture)
Structure	
(Informational) Information Technology Auditing and Review Asset Registration Property Valuation Performance Measurement	(Communicative) Corporatisation Financial Instruments (ditto) (ditto) Commercial Standards
Re-organisation	
Cutting and Reshaping of Expenditure via New Model(s) of Service Provision	
Reform	
Privatisation Responsiveness to Consumer Demand Democratisation	

Figure 2.3   Model of Property Management

The model represents property management in terms of the initiatives and strategies of the informational and communicative structures that underlie the development and which have formed the focus of attention so far. It should be seen as a pedagogical tool: a learning device, useful in the sense it captures the present state of affairs in the development of property management and highlights matters of particular concern. Taking this form the model follows the logic of the examinations carried out in the previous sections of this chapter and the discussions which this has introduced. It identifies the form and content of the initiatives in question and draws attention to the strategies that underpin these particular developments. Having set out the model of property management in Figure 2.3, it is now possible to examine the relationships between the components forming the technical and communicative structures of property management.

The discussion that follows will do this by focussing on the critical nature of the relationships in question. In focussing on the critical nature of the relationships between the said components:

- it is evident that property management can not be restricted to the legal and social structure of tenure, but has to include the economics of the property market underlying the VFM and 3Es of the corporate, financial and commercial dimensions of property asset management;
- the search for efficiency should centre on the exchange of property and, for allocative reasons, include the techniques of analysis capital markets require for the corporate strategies and financial instruments of property management to meet the required commercial standards;
- the role of the corporate and financial dimensions of property management is to extend the logic of capital markets in to the management of property;
- this requires that all property assets are subjected to the logic of capital market pricing;
- the object of the capital market pricing should not be seen as being restricted to exchange per se, but as providing the technical, vis-à-vis allocative efficiencies this process of marketisation in turn introduces;
- this process of marketisation should in turn be seen as providing the means to strategically incorporate this line of reason into the financial instruments and commercial standards required to manage property.

What form of capital market pricing is emerging is illustrated in the contemporary model of property management set out in Figure 2.4. At the centre of this illustration lies the economics of the property market, in terms of VFM and the 3Es of resource allocation along both exchange and technical lines. It is from here the capital markets become the main allocative mechanism regulating how the corporate strategy and financial instruments in question regulate the operational/occupational and investment requirements of property management. It illustrates that under the said strategy and instruments, it is the information systems, data-bases, registers, valuation and both audits and reviews that progress the search for exchange/technical efficiency via the marketisation and analysis their management subjects property to. The forms of market analysis that are shown in the illustration as cash flows, annuities, considerations of risk and uncertainty, discounting etc. and which in turn provide the commercial standards of performance measurement in terms of yields, growth, depreciation and rates of return.

This gives a critical insight into what is meant by property management. It illustrates that while emphasis is placed upon the corporate level, the focus of attention is on the financial, as it is here the exchange/technical efficiencies of the capital markets underlying the analysis of information systems, data-bases, registers and valuations turn into commercial standards of performance measurement. Where the contemporary model outlined here differs from others is in the type of abstractions it proposes ought to be drawn upon for such purposes. The exact point of difference lying in the fact it advocates the use of abstract representations of exchange already available in the social and legal structure of tenure underlying the property market: those to do with the economics of capital pricing, corporate strategy and financial instruments, of, for example; cash-flows, discounting, uncertainty, risk, growth and depreciation. Those strategies and instruments - and this is an important point from the allocative efficiency point of view - whose exchange, techniques of analysis, information systems and data-bases, are common to all forms of property, be they registered as standard, non-standard, specialist, non-specialist, income-producing or cost-generating assets, requiring either the income or cost approach to valuation.

This representation advocates the use of 'tried and tested' abstractions. Tried and tested abstractions that not only form the common currency of exchange in the property market, but which provide the techniques of analysis also qualifying how property should be managed. As such they also represent a collection of abstractions that provide the commercial standards which managers need to measure the performance of the property. Such a representation also has the advantage of avoiding the negative indices associated with simple identity thinking - the situation where property management adds up to little more than the management of income producing assets within the property market. It does this by positing investment not as a thing i.e. an income producing asset, but as a relationship: a relationship that is based in the economics of exchange and the search for techniques of analysis which allow the managers of property to derive efficiencies from the capital markets underlying the corporate strategy and financial instruments that property management rests on. The financial instruments (information systems, data-bases, registration and valuation procedures) that property management rests upon and whose economics of exchange in turn provide the techniques of analysis which make it possible to turn a negative into a positive. Turn a negative in to a positive, by - in this instance - allowing the process of marketisation to effectively bring about the efficiencies and economies such a form of property management seeks to deliver.

It is perhaps because this form of property management is not just exchange-based, but centred on the techniques of capital markets analysis, that it becomes possible to produce the economies and efficiencies which the corporate sector are searching for. The efficiencies that the corporate sector is searching for and which can be found using the financial instruments needed to turn operational assets held for occupational purposes (making up no less than 55 per cent of total UK asset value) into investments. Into investments whose techniques of analysis provide the commercial standards of performance measurement.

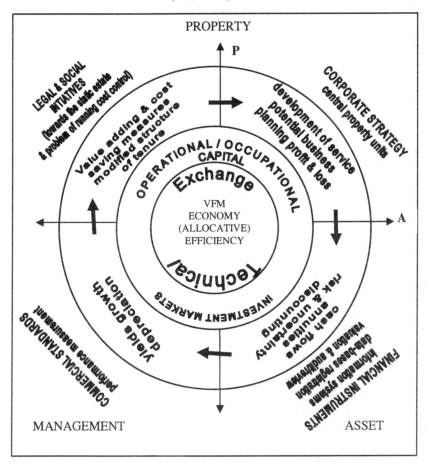

Figure 2.4   The Pro-investment Form of Property (Asset) Management

While providing a critical insight into the nature of the relationships in question, it has to be recognised the examination has tended to focus on the technical structure of property management. As yet little has been said about the communicative structure of property management. The chapters which follow on from this examination will focus on this matter. In the two chapters that follow, attention will turn to the communicative structure of property management. His will be done by focusing on the critical nature of the relationship between the corporate strategies and financial instruments of property management.

Some signposts

Although the task of giving due consideration to the management of property is not an easy one, a number of points can be drawn from the forgoing discussions:

- put into context, the developments in question represent a major challenge and one that is particularly difficult for them to meet due to the fact the Taylorist form of organisation and bureaucratic management of technology, under Fordism and the welfare state, has (during the post-war development of the public sector in particular) tended to be routine, habit forming and centre upon little more than the commercial transactions of buying and selling estates;
- the shift towards the development of initiatives and strategies represents a transition from estate to property management;
- over the decade or so, most headway has been made in the development of initiatives to introduce IT in the registration of assets, valuation of property, audit, review and measurement of performance to meet the VFM test and establish the 3Es;
- in contrast, there has been a noticeable absence of expertise available to assist in the cultural development of both the corporate strategy and financial instruments required to form the framework for such initiatives, tests and criteria;
- it is the financial instruments for the management of property that represent the most problematic issue, for while considerable progress has been made on the registration of property, unease exists over the relationship between the cost and income approaches to valuation (Marshall and Fisher respectively) due to the breakdown of post-war consensus over the technology and economics of the welfare state and inability of the discourse on enterprise and competition to provide either an informational basis or communicative structure which represents an acceptable alternative;
- at present the discourse centres around the financial instruments of valuation and distinction between exchange, use value and income foregone in terms of opportunity cost from the marketisation of property management;
- the notion of opportunity cost is being used to simulate the market, generate cash flows, annuities and capital charges;
- the developments move the transition beyond land audits and property reviews and towards a form of strategic management that represents a deep and thorough re-organisation of property management;
- these developments are not peculiar to the UK but are mirrored by the evolution of corporate real estate management in the USA. In both the UK and USA it is the marketisation of management as applied to property or real estate that is all pervasive and it is this development which is being made use of in the transition from the static estate and problem of running cost control;
- the irony of this lies in the fact it is the tailoring and re-engineering of Ford that is leading the way in the response to what is known as the crisis of Fordism under the welfare state, economic re-organisation and development of

producer services forming part of the transition towards the corporate management of real estate/property as a strategic resource. The tailoring and re-engineering that is in many instances being used as a model for the deep and thorough re-organisation of real estate/property;

- the development of the producer services in question mark a major discursive shift towards a more 'reflexive' understanding based on theoretical knowledge, systems design, modelling and testing (the building of meta-information data-bases and communicative structures as expert systems). It also breaks with the hierarchically divided bureaucracy of standardised service provision in the post-war welfare state and introduces what are termed 'post-Fordist structures', with flatter, more horizontal arrangements, addressing the risk and uncertainties of enterprising, more competitive and decentred-market regimes for the management of property;

- while the developments can be seen as a response to the crisis of Fordism in the welfare state - In the form of the fiscal tightening, cut-back in public expenditure, search for VFM and 3Es under 'zero-sum' budgets, the lack of data currently available on the development makes it difficult to establish whether the initiatives and strategies underlying the emerging high-tech, economic cum cultural paradigm of the information rich and communicative form of property management, represents a drive towards privatisation, improvement in responsiveness, or movement towards the democratisation of property management.

Conclusions

This goes some way to set out the significance of seeing the development of property management as a combination of initiatives and strategies. The issue is also significant for a further reason; for the fact that in dealing with the allocation of resources, it has become an even more salient aspect of property management due in part to the environment of zero sum budgets, funding shortages, capital spending restrictions, standard spending assessments and service cut backs which accompany the new model of service provision. The emphasis here being on the development of corporate strategies and financial instruments by which to administer radical cutbacks, improve responsiveness to consumer demand and a democratisation of service provision. In contrast to the developments referred to so far, this has to be seen as a matter that is of particular significance for the question of re-organisation and reform and represents a terrain which has not yet been mapped out.

Chapter 3

Corporate Strategies

Introduction

The following will review the status of corporate strategies in the management of property. The review will paint a dismal picture of corporate strategy in the management of property. It will then go on examine the corporatisation of property management that has taken place over the past 15 years to tackle the static estate and problem of running cost control. From here attention turns to the central units developed to resolve the problems associated with the management of property. Attention is subsequently drawn to the strategic advantages that central units offer. The review is then drawn to a close by examining the strategic response property managers have taken to provide VFM and the 3Es.

The question of waste

In addressing the question of 'waste' in the expenditure of money on the management of property held by local authorities, the AC (1988a: 7) state:

> It would be wrong to imply that high quality property management cannot be found in local authorities. It can. The Commission's team has encountered some examples of excellent and imaginative property management in the authorities visited. Some of them are detailed in the longer report. Many local government property officers are highly skilled and committed people. But they work in a difficult environment, heavily influenced by the external factors, and often by a fragmented approach to property management within authorities themselves. As a result, property management is not always given the high priority it deserves. This in turn spawns a wide range of management problems, which can be found to a greater or lesser extent in nearly all local authorities.

As the quote points out, while examples of high quality property management can be found in the public sector, property has not received the priority it deserves and as a consequence, has given rise to a 'wide-range' of management problems, found, to a 'greater or lesser' extent in all such organisations. As Weatherhead (1997:20) also goes on to point out, such problems are not confined to the public sector. Commenting on the independent sector, it is noted:

...managers have no idea of the cost of their unit's accommodation, either as a proportion of central costs or in real terms. Research from Hillier Parker (Bannock and Partners, 1994) revealed that most directors could not give a general idea of the sum of the annual real estate costs.

Similar results were found a year later, when a survey for Richard Ellis showed that only half of those contacted claimed to know the costs of rent, heating, lighting and taxes of their offices...

It would seem that it is still common for local managers to be left to make their own decisions as to when real estate is needed. Although a budget will be have been agreed with someone, most frequently this does not relate to a real estate policy or overall strategy.

While alarming to read, it should be recognised the categorisation of property management set out in the quotes is drawn from the most in-depth and extensive study of the subject to date. In-depth and extensive studies, whose categorisation of property management as 'wasteful', suffering from the problems of 'running cost control', has to be taken seriously if the difficulties they present are to be resolved. If, that is, the costs which are associated with the management of property are to be kept under control.

Corporatisation

The key to turning property management around, making it provide VFM and the 3Es, is seen to lie in recognising the fundamental weakness of the corporate strategy adopted for the management of property. For while there is evidence to show property has been subject to a process of corporatisation over the past 15 years, it appears the central units put in place to manage this strategy have failed to realise any tangible benefits. Indeed the representation of property management as wasteful and unable to keep costs under control, suggests that the process of corporatisation and central units which oversee it, do not give VFM, or the 3Es. Furthermore, the said representation suggests the reason for this apparent 'wastefulness' and inability to keep costs under control rests with the inadequate strategies corporations have adopted for managing property.

In seeking to tackle the failure of corporatisation and provide central units with an adequate strategy, it has been proposed that:

- property must be held for a specified purpose;
- property must be seen not as a static, but dynamic resource, the use of which must be subject to audit and continually reviewed in relation to the strategy of the corporation as a whole;
- property users must be aware of, and held responsible for, the opportunity cost of the asset;
- individual properties or groups of properties should be managed on a cost centre basis, with clear identification of the responsibility for control of running costs.

While these proposals may seem obvious, cultivating them requires leadership, determination and patience, because under estate management, it is the service departments that draw upon the expertise of surveyors on matters concerning the acquisition and disposal of land and buildings. In contrast, the position under property management is somewhat different. Under property management the acquisition and disposal of land and buildings has been subject to a process of corporatisation. This in turn develops central units that make sure the strategy which is adopted is not departmental but corporate. Here the authority for the management of property is seen to switch from the department to the central unit. The central unit subsequently becomes responsible for developing a strategy capable of managing property on behalf of the corporation as a whole.

Central units

The examination of property management by Avis, Gibson and Watt (1989) identifies that central units have been set up to develop an appropriate strategic response. Surveying both the independent and public sector's responses to the developments, they provide evidence to suggest that the central units which have been set up take the following forms:

- separate companies for managing property;
- separate service departments within existing corporations, either in the independent or public sector;
- specialist service sectors managing property within wider departments.

The relative distribution of the central units is set out in Table 3.1. What this illustrates is that while in the independent sector it is quite common to see central units take on the form of a separate company, this is not the case in the public sector. It also shows that it is most common to see central units managing property as separate service departments with existing corporations - be they in the independent or public sector. Table 3.1 also indicates that in the public sector it is quite common to see central units take on the form of specialist service sectors in the 'wider' departments of existing corporations. Cutting across the sectors, it is most common to see central units take on the form of separate service departments in companies. The statistics set out in Table 3.1 suggests separate service departments account for approximately 60 per cent of all the central units set up to manage property.

Table 3.1   Central Units

	Independent	Public
Separate company	30%	4%
Separate service department	50%	61%
Specialist service sector within wider department	20%	35%

Avis, Gibson and Watt (1989) also go on to point out: 29 per cent of the central units are headed by general practice surveyors, 26 per cent with engineers, 13 per cent with quantity and building surveyors, the other main category being architects with 12 per cent. As they point out, 39 per cent of all central units are 'headed up' by surveyors responsible for the strategic and routine day-to-day management of property. Avis and Gibson's (1995) survey suggests this figure has now increased to 69 per cent.

As a response to the waste associated with the static estate and problem of running cost control this produces, central units are seen to provide the following advantages:

- it has command over all management matters;
- the unit (as a corporate body) is responsible for the strategic management of property;
- it provides 'arms length' professional advice on the management of property to service department users, directors and executives;
- in introducing a quasi-landlord and tenant structure of tenure, the unit acts for the landlord, with users occupying or in possession of property having their own advisors;
- in taking on such a role, the unit can specify the aims and objectives of the strategy, distinguishing between strategic and routing day-to-day matters;
- it can initiate a survey of holdings to provide an inventory of ownership, users and occupiers;
- the unit can set up the information systems and IT required to charge asset rents under capital accounting procedures;
- it can also draw upon the said information system and IT to support central units in their audit and review of land and property;
- the aforementioned can be drawn upon to design an asset register and categorise holdings so that the operational and investment dimensions of property can be recognised;
- it can also introduce modern accountancy systems required for the valuation of property on the basis of net current replacement cost;

- the valuations can be drawn upon to calculate asset rents and impose capital charges on the use of property;
- such changes are income producing across all categories of property holdings - operational and investment, forming transfer payments from tenant to landlord;
- as a package of initiatives the asset register, property valuations and capital charges, provide the performance measurement standards management adopt to address the static estate and problem of running cost control;
- the introduction of performance measurement allows the management of property to meet the 3Es;
- the technical and economic nature of these initiatives, in turn, allow a pro-quality, enterprise-minded, competitive and accountable strategy to be adopted for the management of property;
- such a strategy is seen to be corporate in the sense that it cultivates a structure of communication which subjects the management of property to a process of corporatisation.

Case-study examples

The following provides some case-study examples of the central units set up to manage property. They provide examples of the central units set up as separate companies, service departments and specialist sectors. The examples in question are those of: Chartwell Land, BT and Marks and Spencers. Each corporation provides a case-study example of central units set up as separate companies (Chartwell Land), separate service departments (BT) and specialist sectors within larger departments (Marks and Spencer).

Chartwell Land

Chartwell Land forms the central unit of the Kingfisher Group (Woolworths, Superdrug and B&Q). As the central unit, Chartwell Land acts as the landlord of the Kingfisher Group managing the property held by its operational units - Woolworths, Superdrug and B&Q. As landlords, Chartwell Land are responsible for the acquisition and disposal of property and management of leases held by Woolworths, Superdrug and B&Q as tenants. Having responsibility for the negotiation of leases, setting of rents, maintenance and repair, Chartwell Land manage the Group's property as an investment. Under this structure of tenure, Chartwell Land are responsible for the Group's investments and managing the property occupied for operational purposes - providing the retail services in question.

The expertise needed to manage the property is divided between the centre and the Group's operational units. The centre is responsible for property investment, while the operational units manage routine matters relating to their occupation.

BT

Following privatisation, BT set up a central unit as a separate service department. As a separate service department, the Group's property management objective is to provide VFM and the 3Es. Unlike the position taken by Chartwell Land, BT's central unit does not take the form of a separate company and because of this, has not sought to superimpose a formal landlord-tenant type structure onto the Group. Rather than developing a structure that allows property to be managed as an investment, BT have sought operational efficiency from operators. This has required a complete overhaul of the Group's operations and rethink of how to manage property. The central unit's response has been not only to manage property as an investment, but as an operational unit occupied for the purpose of delivering services. This central unit has expertise situated within its headquarters and relies heavily on the use of consultants to support BT's management of property.

Marks and Spencer

Like BT, Marks and Spencer's central unit has sought to improve operational efficiency. This has required the central unit to expand their retail operations and rationalise the corporation by divesting the Group of its role in the distribution of goods and services. Unlike BT, the central unit developed by Marks and Spencer has not required a complete overhaul of the Group's operations, or rethink of how to manage property. Again the expertise is located in the organisation's headquarters and much of the property management is contracted out to consultants.

The case studies

Reflecting on these case studies, it is possible to see the development of central units as a means to:

- introduce a landlord-tenant type structure into the management of property held by corporations;
- divide management responsibilities between the investment and operational needs of corporate groups;
- give 'the centre' the authority for managing strategic issues and make operational units responsible for routine matters associated with the occupation of property;
- manage property in a way that gives VFM and the 3Es and which is strategically economic and operationally efficient.

The strategic advantages of central units

The strategic advantages of central units are noticeable and have prompted a number of similar developments from other well known corporations. Table 3.2 shows the range of corporations that have set up central units to manage property. As Table 3.2 illustrates central units for the management of property are now common, can be seen to cut across the standard industrial classification (SIC) and include corporations from the industrial and services sectors. Also noticeable is the fact the additional case-study examples are drawn from both the independent and public sector.

The strategic response

The strategic management of property developed by the said central units is based upon the evidence of 'best practice' from the AC's (1988a,b), Avis, Gibson and Watts' (1995) and Weatherhead's (1997) in-depth and extensive studies of property management. Here attention is drawn to a number of developments in property management and how central units 'piece various initiatives together' to form a strategy for the management of property. The initiatives that are pieced are numerous and are technical, economic and informational in nature. As technical and economic developments in VFM, they represent the following:

- land audits
- property reviews
- marketing exercises and
- information systems set up for charging asset rents under capital accounting and the contracting of services.

As informational developments they include:

- the audit and review of land and buildings;
- registration of assets;
- valuation of property and;
- measurement of performance.

Table 3.2   Case-study Examples

Corporate Sector		
SIC	**Independent**	**Public**
Industrial	Kraft(1)	
	Ford (1)	
	Hewlett Packard (1)	
	IBM(2)	
Services		
(retail)	Boots(3)	
	Marks & Spencer (3)	
	Olivers (3)	
	Sainsbury's (3)	
(transport		
and	BAA (4)	
communication)	BT (3)	
(real estate)	Property Service (5)	
	Kingfisher (5)	
(banking		
and	Barclay's (5)	
public admin.)		
		Crown Estates
		Customs and Excise
		Post Office (5)
		Local Authorities (6)
		Further Education (7)
		Higher Education (8)
		NHS (9)

Sources:
1. Joroff et al (1993)
2. Arnison et al (1990)
3. Weatherhead (1997)
4. Edington (1997)
5. Avis et al (1993)
6. Deakin (1998a, b, 99a)
7. Dent (1997, 98)
8. Headley et al (1999)
9. Heald et al (1996)

Together these initiatives are seen to provide the basis for a strategy to provide the 3Es. Moreover, the said initiatives are seen to develop a strategy that is not only pro-quality minded, enterprise-minded, competitive, decentred and accountable, but which is also corporate. While attractive in the line of reasoning it adopts, some observers of the developments have responded by asking how it is possible to cultivate such a corporatisation? Accepting that the corporatisation of property is pro-quality and enterprise-minded, it is possible to examine the competition, decentralisation, accountability and corporate questions which surround strategic developments of this kind. This is because it is ideas about the virtues of competition, decentralisation, accountability and corporatisation in the communicative structure of property which have to a large degree, been responsible for the corporatisation property management has been subject to over the past 15 years.

Table 3.3   **Property Management**

Variables	**Property Management**	**Corporations**
Competitive	Market criteria	Contracting out, market testing and introduction of internal markets
Decentred	Autonomous trading units, non-hierarchical, with flat, broad structures of decision-making, service- based with customer orientation	Centre-periphery forms of Service delivery
Accountable	Audit and review of income and outgoings expenditure - be it revenue or capital based	Control over budgets and regulation of expenditure to meet pre-determined targets
Corporate	Divisional control over budgeting of some services, with executive body and directorate based on the distinction between strategic management and routine operations	Small number of core staff responsible for policy and strategic issues, who network with larger numbers of project-based and task centred experts employed on service delivery to customers.

In theory the introduction of new metaphors like competition, decentralisation and accountability into the culture of property management are quite uncontroversial. But the question about the communicative structure of property management is more problematic and difficult to resolve because it demands we are more exact in the use of such terms. Table 3.3 shows the variables in question and the relationship they have to property management. Here, competition is seen to surface through the introduction of market criteria into property management. This is secured through the process of contracting-out and market-testing and to some extent by the trading of services via the introduction of internal markets (i.e. in the form of service level agreements). Decentralisation goes on to develop this theme by introducing autonomous trading units, with non-hierarchical, or, flat, broad structures of decision-making. This takes the form of either centre-peripheral forms of service delivery, or forms of service delivery that transfer decision making power from the centre to the periphery and on to the customers. The accountability variable comes into play via the introduction of tighter controls over the budgeting of expenditure. Such control is seen to rest with the executive and directorate responsible for the management of property. The former has particular responsibility for managing the uncertainty and risk that surround the formation of a strategy towards the acquisition, use, development and disposal of property. Together the executive and directorate are responsible for the planning, budgeting and control of expenditure on the management of property.

The question of how it is possible to cultivate such a corporatisation and in turn, develop the financial instruments and commercial standards needed to resolve the problem of running cost control, has not yet been looked at? This question shall be addressed in the next two chapters. The search for an answer to the question will begin under the heading of financial instruments.

Conclusions

This examination has reviewed the status of corporate strategies and painted a dismal picture of their use in the management of property. It has gone onto examine the corporatisation of property management that has taken place over the past 15 years to tackle the problem of running cost control. From here attention turned to the central units which have subsequently been developed to resolve the problems associated with the management of property. In this examination attention turned to the strategic advantages that central units offer and the responses which have recently been taken to make sure property management provides VFM and the 3Es.

Chapter 4

Financial Instruments

Introduction

This chapter examines the development of the financial instruments (land audits, property reviews, information systems, registers and approaches to valuation) required to replace 'expenditure-driven finance' with a new system of capital accounting. The examination draws upon the findings of a research project undertaken to survey the initiatives that have taken to develop the asset registers and property valuation procedures for such purposes. The examination goes some way to highlight the critical role property valuation plays in introducing a system of capital accounting which transforms the financing of expenditure and subjects the management of property to VFM and the 3Es.

The question of accountability

> If local authorities are to become fully accountable for their capital expenditure and if [property] managers are to operate [economically and] efficiently, being fully aware of the current costs of the assets they are using, then a new system is required.

The quote appears on the first page of CIPFA's (1989) *Capital Accounting in Local Authorities: The Way Forward*. Prepared by a Joint Steering Group, made up of representatives of the Department of Environment, AC and CIPFA. The document proposes that the public sector should adopt a new system of financial statements and accounting. One that does away with the pre-occupation property managers have with statements about the methods of financing capital expenditure, rather than system of accounting. The position in the independent sector is again set out by Weatherhead (199: 98), who points out:

> many directors do not know the value of their real estate.

At first sight, the proposal to draw a distinction between finance and accounting may appear a little odd. However, on reflection, the reason for this becomes clear: it is because finance in general and within the corporations having responsibility for the provision of services in particular, has previously been driven by expenditure methods rather than accounting systems. The tendency ot focus on the former at the expense of the latter, going some way to explain why 'many directors do not know the vlaue of their real estate'. Indeed it might be said that the tendency to focus attention on methods of financing, rather than a system of accounting for expenditure, is something which exposes the weakness of the present situation and highlights the need to replace the existing expenditure-driven logic of finance with a new system of capital accounting.

The new system of capital accounting

In going on to make the case for the new system of capital accounting, it is proposed that it should be judged on the advantages it has over the expenditure driven logic of finance. In going on to argue the case for capital accounting, attention is drawn to the weaknesses of the expenditure driven logic currently in place. The weaknesses in question are presented as follows:

- the method of financing capital expenditure: for example; by debt, sale and leaseback and receipts, fix the charges to the service department rather than the corporation;
- the result is an arbitrary set of charges, with normal charges for debt, reduced payments for sale and leaseback and no charge for capital expenditure funded from receipts;
- under this formula all charges are paid from the service department revenue accounts and may appear an unusually high burden, or of little consequence, depending on whether capital expenditure is funded by debt or receipt;
- such a formula operates on a 'method driven logic' of expenditure, with different payments, time horizons, economic lives, profiles of obsolescence and depreciation and can penalise one service department budget relative to another;
- this imbalance is compounded due to the fact charges are based on historic, rather than the current cost of replacing the capital in question.

Given the size and scale of the expenditure, it is proposed that such a subjective criteria for the investment of capital is inappropriate. The first point of criticism relates back to the notion of the static estate and observed mis-matches of land and buildings relative to the demands of service departments. Here much emphasis is placed upon, not the need to finance additional expenditure, but to carry out an audit of land, buildings, plant and machinery and in that sense, review of the property which is held by service departments to establish whether it is both 'fit for purpose' and does not lead to the problem of 'running cost control'. This point leads on to the second issue and reflects the concern that any misunderstanding about the purpose of a land audit and property review - be they demographic, technical or economic in nature, may, under the finance driven logic of capital expenditure, lead to additional debt funding and a higher level of costs on repair and maintenance, energy cleansing and insurance, without any commensurate increase in the quality of service provision. While unfortunate, this outcome is seen to be a logical expression of the expenditure driven logic to finance due to the fact the decision to invest does not take account of the opportunity that exists to audit capital expenditure on land, buildings, plant and machinery and review the property which is held by service departments.

It is this land audit and review of property that is seen as pivotal to the switch from finance to accounting because it provides the opportunity to both test and assess not only whether the expenditure of capital adds value, but if it reduces the costs of service provision. To achieve this it is proposed that all capital expenditure should be subject to an audit of land held for service provision and a review of property made use of for such purposes. The former allowing expenditure on capital in the form of land, buildings, plant and machinery for the provision of services, on condition the property held for such purposes is made the subject of a review. The object of this being to review property holdings with a 'view to' identifying any excess capacity in service provision resulting from the expenditure of capital and having any under-used land, building, plant and machinery declared surplus to requirements. The result of this being to have any excess capacity, under-used land, building, plant and machinery declared surplus to requirements and disposed of on an the market, thereby generating a capital receipt to 'balance' any expenditure and offset costs in terms of reduced debt, energy, cleansing and insurance payments.

This switch to 'accounting for capital expenditure' by audit and review is in line with government policy on the 'tightening up' of capital expenditure and its proposal to introduce VFM and the 3Es as a means to achieve this. To achieve this it is proposed the system of capital accounting should recognise that the financing of expenditure is about the corporatisation of property management and the culture of the strategy adopted to meet the 3Es.

If the experience of 'corporatisation' is to mirror that of finance under a 'new system', the logic of capital accounting (its strategic culture) has to illustrate clear advantages over those referred to as methods of financing. Assuming the argument for the corporatisation of property holds for finance and the organisation of a central unit can account for capital expenditure, the advantages of the strategic culture underlying the new system are seen to lie in the following:

- the removal of command over the financing of capital expenditure from service departments to central units as corporate bodies, provides the opportunity to carry out an audit and review on a standard system of accounting;
- such a standard system of accounting, taking the form of VFM tests and 3Es assessments, cuts across departments and gives corporate bodies an organisation wide view of the finance available for capital expenditure on departmental services;
- the system of capital accounting makes it possible for central units to become pro-quality and enterprise-minded by making money the standard measure of value in the test and assessment of economy, efficiency and effectiveness;

- under this strategy the significance of finance becomes apparent with service departments becoming 'rivals', competing with one another for a scarce resource;
- the introduction of current cost accounting on the value of capital replacement allows rivalry and competition to take place on an equal footing, by replacing the anachronisms of historic costs with the decentralised market regime of the present situation and charging both notional interest and depreciation on the capital value of property held by service departments;
- as such, capital charges will only be equal to, or below those paid under the existing system, because of the 'zero-sum', 'below the line' rule for the financing of capital expenditure under this system of accounting.

In responding to the advantages of this format, it is pointed out that there are three issues which have to be addressed if the transfer to the new system is to develop. They are as follows:

- the need for an inventory of assets under the ownership of an organisation as a corporate body with command over the financing of capital expenditure;
- the requirement for a valuation of property under the control of central units and held as assets by departments in connection with service provision;
- the need for the capital charges calculated on the basis of such valuations and additional payments for maintenance and repair, energy, cleansing and insurance to represent the 'full' economic cost of expenditures flowing from the property.

Asset registers

On the question of asset registers, it is acknowledged that the long tradition of cadastras and terriers in estates departments means that much of the information required for the inventory already exists. The question is what form should the property register take? In addressing this question, it is possible to identify three forms of register: manual, low-level and high-level computer based information systems for such purposes. In connection with this matter, the information requirements are defined as core, intermediate and transient data sets on modules, ranging from general information to specific pieces of data of a more specialist kind.

As data-bases, it is proposed registers of this kind should act as information systems whose value ought to lie in the communication they facilitate between central units and service departments - the communication, exchange and transfer of data required to inform managers about the financial situation over the valuation of capital, payment of charges and other such expenditures falling under the terms of reference for audit and review. It is here where the new system of capital accounting is seen to replace the financing of expenditure. This is because it is here with the data-based system of information flow, transfers and communication, that central units not only get the authority to regulate and control the capital expenditure of service departments, but also the financial instruments required for such purposes.

It is at this point the proposal comes full circle and the situation arises where it is the system of capital accounting and its requirements that determine not only the underlying rational of the valuations and capital charges, but the instruments available to finance the expenditure of service departments under VFM and the 3Es. Given none of this can 'go ahead' without the inventory of property and compilation of a register, it is not surprising this matter has attracted a considerable amount of attention, prompting surveys on the form, content and progress made in the movement towards a new system of capital accounting and development of the financial instruments required to regulate and control expenditure (see Deakin, 1998a,b, c, 99a).

Property valuation

For valuation purposes, property falls into the following groups:

- non-operational property (i.e. investment, surplus and development property) is valued on the basis of (Open) Market Value (MV/OMV);
- operational, non-specialised property, valued on the basis of Existing Use Value (EUV); and,
- operational, specialised properties, valued on the basis of DRC.

The valuations are for inclusion in the financial statements of the corporation under the system of capital accounting and to provide a basis for the assessment of charges for the use and consumption of property.

The application of the income approach to the valuation of non-operational, non-specialised property appears to have been met with little controversy. It is the application of the cost approach to the valuation of property and assessment of the current value in terms of replacement, that has been the main cause of concern. While the approach has been studied in depth by Britton, Connellan and Crofts (1991), the basis of valuation i.e. assessment of current value in terms of depreciated replacement cost has raised a number of methodological questions about how to undertake such a valuation of property and the reliability of the determination. The criticisms are as follows:

- the technical nature of the assessment;
- the assumptions regarding useful economic life;
- the treatment of obsolescence and depreciation;
- the assumption on viability of the use;
- the use of notional interest and depreciation as capital charges reflecting the economic cost of use and consumption;
- the use of the latter to represent the rental payment.

Such criticisms do, to some extent, have to be seen as an inevitable consequence of a basis of valuation for property that 'fails to meet the market test'. Fails, that is, because its specialised and non-standard nature means it is not traded on the property market - the main source of reliable evidence as to the current value and price. As in any other situation, the benefits of such valuation have to be balanced against the criticisms. On this point, it is perhaps best to bear in mind that with specialist operational property there is no other form of valuation. It might even be said that in such situations it is the market not the form of valuation that 'fails' and this is why the income approach cannot be applied. In short, it is because an assessment of current value cannot be made of the basis of income and may only be made on the cost approach. Indeed in this situation it is perhaps fair to suggest the failure of the market is also reflected in the income approach and its inability to provide valuations in the absence of property markets.

Looked at in this way, the failure in question is not one of 'the market' but of property and inability of the income approach to appreciate the relationship cost-based valuations also have to capital markets: one which results in both approaches to the valuation of property 'overlapping' in the form of the income's comparative-investment link and the connection the cost approach has to the contractor's and investment method. What is perhaps also important to recognise is that far from being a tactical error, this failure, or inability to appreciate the relationship both have to capital markets is of strategic significance. This is because if we can accept investment is not transaction-based, but grounded in the capital markets underlying the exchange of property, it is the structure of valuation that has to be seen as providing the platform for the income and cost approach. The structure of valuation and platform of income and cost upon which the investment of capital rests.

The value of taking such a perspective on the matter rests in the ability such a representation has to dispense with the idealisation of the 'property market', the notion of evidence to support the 'market test' and definition of 'no-market' properties the income approach to the valuation of investment places so much weight on. For what such a representation does is to transcend the transaction-based logic of the income approach by grounding our understanding of investment in the capital markets underlying the exchange of property: the capital markets that give rise to the structure of valuation and platform upon which both the income and cost approach to property valuation, investment, rent, yields, interest and other such returns charged on the use and consumption of land, buildings, plant and machinery, rest. The significance of this lies in the fact that if we accept it is not property, but capital markets which underlie the exchange in question and gives rise to the structure of valuation, the notion of the 'market-test' and 'no-market' property put forward by advocates of the income approach as a criticism of the cost approach to valuation become irrelevant. This is because in this situation it is the capital markets underlying the exchange of property that gives rise to the structure of valuation in both income and cost terms and constructs the platform upon which investment rests. Under this situation it is evident that it is irrelevant to draw any distinction between the income and cost approaches to valuation on the idea of a 'market-test' or 'no market' property. Both share the same market, pass the test and as a consequence, represent a structure of valuation - be it income or cost, that cannot be described as being for either market or 'no-market' property. Accepting this, it follows that any distinction between the income and cost approach to the valuation of property cannot be based on the failure to pass the market test, or the difference between market and no-market property.

The significance of capital markets

In light of what has just been said, any distinction between the income and cost approach to valuation can no longer be seen as fundamental i.e. to lie with the nature of the property - however defined, or either the absence or presence of markets, but with the methods, techniques and practices of the income and cost approach to property valuation. Not, that is, with the question of markets underlying the exchange of property, or the structure of valuation, but the methods and techniques of market exchange making up both the income and cost approach to property valuation. Put in slightly different terms: with the economics of property valuation and capital markets of the income and cost approach.

If we substitute the words financial instruments and commercial standards for methods and techniques of market exchange, the object of this digression into the theory of property valuation should become clear. It is to highlight the fact that it is not so much the legal or social basis of transactions which determine the exchange of property, as the capital markets which form the basis of the financial instruments and commercial standards in question. That is, give rise to the methods and techniques of market exchange which structure valuation and give rise to the income and cost approach as a platform, not only for investment, rent, yields, interest and other such charges, but VFM and the 3Es in the management of property. This is because in the absence of such instruments i.e. information systems and IT as databases for the audit, review, registration and valuation of property by the income and cost approach, the following would result:

- the 'all-pervasive' marketisation thesis would be severely limited as it would be without the technology and economics required to test for VFM, or the cultural components of the pro-quality, enterprise-minded, competitive, decentred (in this instance capital) market regime, required to make sure the management of property is accountable in terms of the 3Es;
- the corporatisation of property management would be restricted to operational (non-specialist) and investment, or surplus holdings i.e. to those sectors where a market is 'understood' to exist in conventional terms. While this would allow the development of information systems and IT as data-bases for the audit, review, registration of assets and valuation or property, such instruments would merely reproduce the 'status quo' and be unable to draw upon either the methods or instruments of market exchange also representative of the specialist operational sector: unable; in that sense, to cut across the categories

of holding to make sure the market exchange, VFM and 3Es of the 'others' also apply to the specialist operational holdings;

- while in this instance a comprehensive data-base may result, the structure of valuation will still be divided in the absence of general market exchange;
- the absence of a general market in and across all categories, means that while the income approach will produce a rationalisation of property (reallocation of resources) via the disposal of non-operational holdings as defined as surplus to requirements, the failure to accept the authority the cost approach also has to represent the market, results in a situation where the structure of valuation (the income and cost approach to property valuation) is unable to provide the platform required to transform the 'financing of expenditure'. Transform it, that is, into a system of capital accounting which gives rise to charges introducing market disciplines such as rent, yields, interest etc. as the commercial standards of performance measurement and in so doing, make it possible for the management of property to meet both the VFM test and 3Es assessments.

The significance of this development cannot be underestimated as it indicates the transformation of finance from expenditure to capital accounting (under the information systems and IT acting as data-bases for the audit, review, registration and valuation of property), is taking place on a set of financial instruments and commercial standards whose performance measurement conforms to the VFM test and 3 E assessments set out for such purposes. This transformation might also be seen as significant for the fact the development manages to circumvent the idealisations of the property market and transform the financing of expenditure through the introduction of capital accounting, whose information systems, IT, data-bases, audit and reviews, asset registers and structure of valuation (i.e. instruments) act as a platform for the disciplines of market exchange. The disciplines of market exchange leading to commercial standards of performance measurement in the management of property. As such it also indicates that the development of the information systems and IT (as data-bases for the audit, review, registration of assets and valuation of property by central units) in question, is not a paper exercise, but one which reflects the outside pressure which the market is placing upon surveyors to corporatise the management of property. This is something that requires them to adopt a set of financial instruments and commercial standards for the measurement of performance.

Conclusions

The significance of this development in the registration and valuation of property cannot be underestimated. As this examination indicates, the transformation of expenditure under the new system of capital accounting is developing the financial instruments (information systems, data-bases, asset registers, valuation, audit of land and review of property) needed to put management on a commercial footing. The development might also be seen as significant because the transformation circumvents the idealisations of the property market and manages to introduce a system of capital accounting whose information systems, data-bases, asset registers and structure of valuation, also provide a firm platform for the management of property.

Chapter 5

Computer-based Information Systems, Property Management and the Appraisal of Land and Buildings in the Urban Environment

Introduction

Recent reports by the Audit Commission (AC, 1988a, b, c, d, 2000) and Chartered Institute of Public Finance Accountants (CIPFA,1989, 1991a,b, 1993, 1994), all draw attention to the potential computer-based information systems have to improve standards of property management. Yet despite the attention such reports have drawn to the development of computer-based information systems, there is a tendency for studies of this kind to do little more than provide a list of how the application of IT can improve the management of property.

In the interests of focusing attention on the application of IT and development of computer-based information systems for property management, the following will first of all set out the issues in question. It will then go on to look at the theory and method of property management. Attention will then turn to the application of such knowledge and the technology of computer-based information systems. Here attention will focus on the information requirements, IT needs and question of how information systems of this kind bring about an improvement in the management of property. It will then go on to examine what such a system of asset registration, property valuation and performance measurement (referred to collectively as property management), contributes to the appraisal of land and buildings in the urban environment.

Issues

Contrary to the positive image of property management put forward by the AC and CIPFA, there is evidence to suggest the vision of property management as competitive, decentred, accountable and corporate, is fraught with problems. Evidence is emerging to suggest the IT needed to develop the computer-based information systems capable of bringing about such a form of property management does not exist and the absence of such technology is tending to cast some doubt on the ability to meet the standards of property management set out by the AC, CIPFA and Royal institution of Chartered Surveyors (RICS, 1984). The evidence in question tends to suggest the problems and difficulties being encountered with the application of IT and development of computer-based information systems for the management of property, are as follows and lie in:

- the lack of data available on the development of computer-based information systems (Spicer, 1979; Kirkwood, 1984);
- the low level of IT-related skills in the management of property (RICS, 1984; MAC, 1985; Avis, Gibson and Watts, 1989);
- the absence of suitable guidance on the application of IT for the development of computer-based information systems (Dixon, 1985; Ralphs and Wyatt, 1999);
- concern over the design of data-bases as information systems for the management of property (Jenkins and Gronow, 1989; Deakin 1997a, b, 1998a);
- questions about the relationship between such information systems and the asset register (Webster, Gronow and Jenkins, 1995, Deakin,1997a, b, 1998a, b, c);
- unease about the bases of property valuation put forward by the AC and CIPFA (Dent and Bond, 1993; Young, 1995; Dent 1997; Deakin,1999a);
- reservations about the application of income and cost conventions to the valuation and pricing of property (Britton, Connellan and Crofts, 1989, 1991; Connellan,1994, 1998; Martindale, 1994, 1998; Deakin, 1994, 1998a, b, c, d, e, f, g, 1999a,);
- worries over the lack of any clear standards for the measurement of property performance (Crofts, 1989; Gammans, 1990; French, 1994, Carter, 1999; Deakin, 1999b);
- the noticeable absence of any information in terms of the corporate strategy or financial instruments required to improve the standards of property management (Gibson, 1985, 1994; Kirkwood and Padden, 1988; Deakin, 1998b, c, 1999a, b, c, d, e).

As Spicer (1979) and Kirkwood's (1984) observations go some way to show, prior to the AC's reports on property management, questions about the application of IT and development of computer-based information systems attracted little attention. As both Spicer (1979) and Kirkwood (1984) point out, the origins of IT applications in the development of computer-based information systems lie in the Gazetter and Local Authority Management Information Systems (LAMIS). Data-bases that Kirkwood (1984) notes, have been designed not so much with the question of property in mind, as for the management of information having a bearing on the financial planning, budgeting and development of expenditures on public services. Designed, that is, not so much with the property manager as information officer in mind.

This is an unfortunate situation the RICS (1984) and Management Analysis Centre (MAC, 1985) also draw attention to and see as directly responsible for the low level of IT skills available to assist organisations in the management of property. It is a view also supported to a large degree by Dixon (1989) and Avis, Gibson and Watts' (1989) discussions about the problems and difficulties being experienced over the lack of suitable guidance on the development of computer-based information systems, design of data-bases and adoption of software for the registration of assets, valuation of property and measurement of performance (see also, for example; Jenkins and Gronow 1989; French, 1994 and Martindale, 1995 on the respective issues).

As a set of separate issues, the problem and difficulties listed give obvious cause for concern. The lack of data, low level of IT skills and absence of suitable guidance, all tend work against any attempts to apply IT in the development of computer-based information systems. Perhaps most noticeable of all is the extent and nature of the problems and difficulties property managers face in attempting to apply IT in the development of such information systems. For in looking at the list of concerns, questions, general level of unease, reservations and worries in question, it is evident the problems and difficulties are not self contained, or isolated to any one issue; for example: the application of IT, development of computer-based information systems, registration of assets, valuation of property, or measurement of performance, but are inter-related to one another. This is most noticeable in the absence of guidance, concern over the design of databases and questions about the relationship between such information systems and the registration of assets. For not only does this represent a problem in its own right, but one that also causes difficulties in the form of unease, reservations and worries about the valuation of property and measurement of performance.

The structure of property management

Looked at together, it is also evident that such an array of problems and difficulties signal something more significant and tends to indicate the cause for concern does not lie with any one issue, but with the structure of property management as a whole. That is with both the initiatives and strategies of property management which surveyors have adopted to guide them in the application of IT and development of computer-based information systems.

To test this hypothesis, it will of course be necessary to examine the structure of property management and assess how well the initiatives and strategies of property management translate into in the application of IT and development of computer-based information systems. As should become clear from the review of the developments that have already taken place, if anything there has been a tendency for computer-based information systems to take on the status of asset registers, rather than tools for the valuation of property and measurement of performance. Something this examination shall suggest is unfortunate and needs to be overcome if the limits it places on the valuation of property and measurement of performance are to be addressed. If, that is, the application of IT in the development of computer-based information systems is to improve the standards of property management along the lines which have been set out by the AC, CIPFA and RICS.

The new model of service provision

There are perhaps four main variables in the pro-quality, enterprise-minded vision of property management and few constants. The variables are competition, decentralisation, accountability and corporatisation. It is the ideas about the virtues of competition, decentralisation, accountability and corporatisation in the communicative structure, which have brought about a re-organisation and reform property management. What the new - competitive, decentralist, accountable and corporate - model of service provision represents, is an attempt to cut and reshape expenditure on the management of property and in turn re-organise and reform property management as part of the search for better standards.

Table 5.1   Property Management and Corporations

Variables	Property Management	Corporations
Competitive	Market criteria	Contracting out, market testing and introduction of internal markets
Decentred	Autonomous trading units, non-hierarchical, with flat, broad structures of decision-making, service- based with customer orientation	Centre-periphery forms of service delivery
Accountable	Audit and review of income and outgoings expenditure - be it revenue or capital based	Control over budgets and regulation of expenditure to meet pre-determined targets
Corporate	Divisional control over budgeting of some services, with executive body and directorate based on the distinction between strategic management and routine operations	Small number of core staff responsible for policy and strategic issues, who network with larger numbers of project-based and task centred experts employed on service delivery to customers.

In theory the introduction of new metaphors like competition, decentralisation and accountability into the culture of property management are quite uncontroversial. But the question about the communicative structure of property management is more problematic and difficult to resolve because it demands we are more exact in the use of such terms. In view of this the following shall break the question down into three parts. The first concentrates on what action needs to be taken if property management is to become competitive, decentralist, accountable and corporate. The second draws upon these terms of reference to provide a more detailed framework for the management of property. The third draws attention to the steps that need to be taken if such a form of property management is to develop. The third point should bring us back to the questions about the technology of computer-based information systems.

Action that needs to be taken

Table 5.1 shows the variables in question and the relationship they have to property management. Here, competition is seen to surface through the introduction of market criteria into property management. This being secured through the process of contracting-out and market-testing and to some extent by the trading of services via the introduction of internal markets (i.e. in the form of service level agreements). Decentralisation goes on to develop this theme by introducing autonomous trading units, with non-hierarchical, or, flat, broad structures of decision-making. This takes the form of either centre-peripheral forms of service delivery, or forms of service delivery that transfer decision making power from the centre to the periphery and on to the customers.

Table 5.2 attempts to highlight how the four principles referred to so far as variables become part of property management. How, that is, the principles become 'incorporated' into the management of property and way in which they take on a particular form. It shows that it is the formation of a central unit which makes it possible to transfer authority for the management of such resources to an executive. It also illustrates that it is the setting up of controls and budgetary planning mechanisms to standards set by independent bodies which allows the VFM test to be taken into account and establish whether service delivery benefits from the 3Es. Here decentralisation takes place via the break-up of departments into a network of autonomous 'trading' units. An event made possible by the development of information systems linking the centre to the periphery through the authority the unit gives an executive to develop a strategy towards the ownership, use, acquisition, disposal and development of property and it in turn gives the directorate to manage routine operations. The execution, direction, financial planning and budgeting of such a strategy is also seen to take place in a competitive environment due to the adoption of market testing and contracting.

Table 5.2   Property Management in Corporations

Property	Management
Corporate	Central unit responsible for policy formation and strategy for the management of property through an executive and directorate
Accountability	Application of IT to control expenditure on the management of property and to meet pre-determined targets and standards set by independent bodies
Decentralisation	Delegation of decision making power via network of communications to and from autonomous trading units and made possible by the development of computer-based information systems linking the centre to peripheral activities
Competition	Through the adoption of market testing, contracting out, financial criteria for the registration on assets, valuation of property and measurement of performance (by unit comparison of income, outgoings and rates of return) on commercial standards

Fortunately, it is possible to see how this model is applied in practice by reference to a number of studies undertaken to monitor the development of property management. It should be noted that the studies are limited to the asset registration stage of development. For the purpose of this paper the fact that the information available is limited to the initial stages of the development is not something which raises problems for as should become clear, it serves to pin-point a problem of particular concern. As already pointed out, the development of information systems for the registration of assets is an aspect of property management the AC and CIPFA have drawn particular attention to. As a general rule neither institution has sought to be prescriptive in laying down the type of system organisations should adopt and have simply suggested it ought to develop 'fitness for purpose' in terms of fulfilling this particular function.

In the first attempt to monitor the development of such information systems, the ADC (1990) found that while many local authorities have introduced IT into the management of property, some have been successful in this venture but others have failed. In a subsequent exercise aimed at surveying the types of information systems in place, Erdman Lewis (1993) found that 75 per cent of local authorities had introduced computer-based information systems for the management of property. Out of this, 39 per cent were found to take the form of mainframe databases, 36 per cent microprocessor, or personal computer based. The survey also highlighted that a great many organisations perceive the value of the information systems to lie in the ability data-bases have to act as an electronic filing cabinet, holding information about property in the form of data on ownership, tenure, use, value and the cost of outgoings. In effect in the ability computer-based information systems of this kind have to act as a register of assets. One that not only provides data in the form of an asset register, but information valuable for the next stage of the management process i.e. the valuation of property and measurement of performance.

It is the perception of computer-based property information systems as little more than electronic filing cabinets, capable of speeding up the access to data held on assets which this examination seeks to avoid. Indeed it is hoped that the discussions which have taken place so far have already gone some way in achieving this. In contrast, it seeks to adopt a wider definition and one that places emphasis, not so much on the capacity for systems of this kind to operate as a data bank, but on the information they provide for the next stage of the management process. It also adopts such a definition in an attempt to transcend the rather narrow view of information systems as data banks for the registration of assets and in the aim of drawing particular attention to the data and information required for the valuation of property and measurement of performance. It is also adopted because such a tripartite definition of property management provides the key to recognising the pivotal role computer-based information systems play in the strategic and routine operation of management functions.

The technology of computer-based information systems

So far attention has focused on a number of problems and difficulties associated with the development of property management and how the theory and method of the aforesaid tends to result in computer-based information systems being seen as little more than data-banks: a perception this examination argues is far too narrow and fails to address the questions of property valuation and performance measurement - the other two dimensions of the management function.

Here the discussion will move beyond the consideration of theory and method and shall consider the technology of computer-based information systems. In focusing on the technology of computer-based information systems, the examination aims to show what measures can be taken to overcome the difficulties and problems in the theory and method of property management outlined so far. In meeting this objective the discussion will divide into three parts: the information requirements, the IT needs, system design and operation.

Information requirements

As all discussions on the application of IT to the management of property tend to point out, before considering the technology of computer-based information systems, it is first necessary to specify what information is required. Keeping this maxim firmly in mind, the development in question identified the following requirements:

- a central unit, who in conjunction with an executive and directorate will be responsible for the strategy;
- an executive with responsibility for strategy towards the corporatisation of property in terms of: the acquisition, use, development and disposal of holdings and direction of more routine operations concerning their management;
- a computer-based information system capable of providing the corporate body with the financial instruments required to control expenditure on the management of property - be they operational, investment, or assets held surplus to requirements on the trading account;
- data for the registration of assets on the computer-based information system, manipulation of data and processing of information for the valuation of property and measurement of performance under the said corporatisation and set of financial instruments;
- a network of communications to link the property management division to the user of assets.

As Figure 5.1 shows, it is the formation of a central unit that makes it possible to develop a strategy that 'corporatises' the acquisition, use, development and disposal of property. This being done through the division of management responsibilities between the executive and directorate (as a corporate body). The former having responsibilities for the strategic aspects of property in terms of use, development and disposal, the latter directing the more routine management operations. It also illustrates the question about whether property passes the 'VFM test', or if the management of holdings meets the '3Es', are answered through the corporatisation of property management and financial instruments developed to control expenditure in line with the commercial standards laid down by independent bodies. What it also illustrates is that decentralisation takes place through the delegation of decision-making power into what can be best referred to as a 'network of communications' to and from autonomous trading units. Communications made possible by the development of computer-based information systems linking the centre i.e. central unit, to the executive, directorate and client-customer 'interface', via the circulation of information also required for the valuation of property and measurement of performance. The valuation of property and measurement of performance, making up the financial instruments and commercial standards of property management.

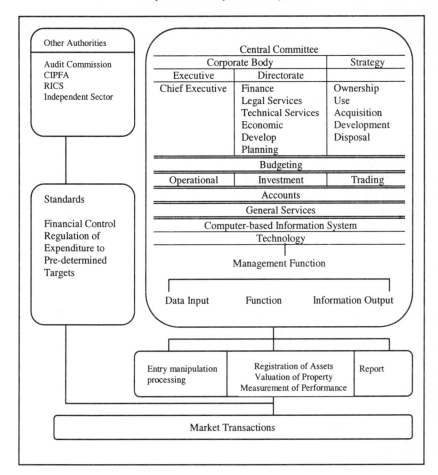

Figure 5.1   Information Requirements

The diagram also attempts to highlight how the four principles referred to so far as 'variables' (i.e. competitive, decentralised, accountable and corporate) become part of property management. How, that is, they become strategically incorporated into a culture of property management emerging under this new model of service provision. For as can be seen, at the centre of the development there is the unit, with a corporate body, directorate and assigned strategy towards the control and budgeting of expenditure on the operational, investment and trading accounts. In this instance, commercial, industrial and residential categories of property. Below this is the computer-based information system linking property to the technology required to fulfil the so-called management function.

While the diagram goes some way to show the pivotal role the computer-based information system takes in the management of property under such a structure, it also identifies the points of contact where it:

- 'incorporates' the variables referred to earlier under the new model of service provision. For as can be seen, it is the relationship between the type of information draw upon and the structure property management that is critical to meeting the competitive criteria. The fact, that is, it draws upon data from market transactions, which is then made use of as information for the valuation of property and measurement of performance;
- introduces information systems which allow a more decentred decision making process for the management of property. One whose application of IT is also seen to be more accountable in the way it transfers authority for the management of property away from the departments responsible for the direct provision of services, to a central unit - a situation that in effect vests the ownership and control of property in a central unit, which in turn allocates responsibility for both the strategic and routine aspects of the management function to an executive and directorate.

Experience suggests it is best to simplify the information requirements by dividing them into the following categories:

- information regarding legal status, ownership, use, holding purpose etc., from existing, usually card index and manual-based property records;
- plan drawings, site, floor areas from land survey, along with engineering, construction, building design, repair and maintenance details supplied by technical services;
- tenure details regarding the allocation of property rights to service departments from legal services, with class of asset, category, holding purpose i.e. operational, investment or on the trading account held surplus to requirements, along with rents, market yields and transfer prices;
- data from intermediate and service departments on outgoings including energy, cleansing, repair and maintenance, insurance, local tax and management costs.

Having obtained the data, consideration has to be given to how it can best represent the material suitable for input into a computer-based information system. In doing this it is considered best not to focus on the IT upon which the computer is based, but on the information system that is required to move the management process from one stage to another. In view of this, it is perhaps best to organise the information in such a way that it allows the exercise to progress through the following stages:

- survey (data collection) for audit and review purposes;
- the registration, entry of the specified data to input the physical, legal and financial attributes of assets;
- manipulation and processing of data for the valuation of property;

- further processing of data to provide information for the measurement of performance;
- reporting on the management of property.

IT needs

The application of IT in the design of the information system in question has taken place on the assumption it should be geared towards meeting user needs. In this instance, the property manager's needs regarding the development of a computer-based information system for the registration of assets, valuation of property and measurement of performance (see Hsia and Bryne, 1989). Taking into account the comments made earlier about the absence of IT expertise in the field of property management, it is perhaps best to try and meet the users' requirements through the adoption of what is commonly referred to as the 'toolbox' approach to systems design. That is not by the commissioning of a 'bespoke', or 'tailor made' information system, but through the design, operation and maintenance of a computer-based information system which makes use of a micro-processor and data-base with auxiliary software.

The advantages of taking such an approach to the system design are numerous and include the following:

- the relatively low level of skill they require for the design, operation and use of information systems;
- the fact that personal computers are relatively cheap and readily available;
- the software is also readily available and inexpensive;
- it is possible to 'customise' the data-base files and structure of records to function as a information system for the management of property;
- the information system is flexible and can be modified to meet changing circumstances;
- it is also relatively user-friendly, with easy to follow menus, screen layouts, data retrieval commands and report writing;
- auxiliary software allows more complex tasks to be undertaken.

As Kirkwood (1984) points out, the use of micro-processors as the computational basis of an information system has the distinct advantage of allowing the mass storage of data and making it possible to quickly process information - it is also seen to provide users with a high quality output that is both reliable and accurate (also see, Hsia, 1989). As Dixon, Hargitay and Bevan (1991) point out, micro-computers of this kind i.e. with a data-base and software package, have the district advantage of providing data-base management systems capable of mirroring LAMIS, but without the considerable cost of a bespoke mainframe technology.

Design and operation

Figure 5.2 shows the design of the computer-based information system. It breaks the structure of the system down into columns of: microcomputer, database, software and function. The form and content of the system require further explanation.

Micro-computer	*Data-base*	*Software*	*Functions*
Fileserver, with network on token ring	*Design* of files, structure of screen layout and records	DBase II - V	*Survey* of property using proformas
Individual personal computers	*Input* of primary data and secondary data on current values from the property and construction sector		Audit and review, via the *registration* of assets' physical, legal and financial attributes
Database held on file server where processing takes place before being sent to PC's.	Data manipulation, sorting, indexation, calculation *processing*, functions, command and programming facilities, data output in the form of reports	*Word processor (with memo fields) spread-sheet applications* (Lotus 1-2-3 for Windows, Microsoft Excel) *Statistical packages* (Super Calc 5)	*Valuation of property* by classifications, base, category of holding and sector
			Performance measurement, in terms of costs of outgoings, yields, risk, growth, obsolescence and depreciation, rate of return over cost

Figure 5.2   Design of the Computer-based Information System

The design of the files and structure of the screen layout set the parameters for the survey and proformas used to input data. In addition to providing the record, or data on the property in question, it also forms the basis of the asset register through the input of data provided from the survey of each holding. Following on from the question of design and data input, are those of processing and information manipulation for the valuation of property. The processing and information for the valuation of property draws upon two data sources: the register for the assets forming the subject of valuation and the property transaction file. The latter holding information on unit rates in the property and construction sector and evidence of current values from transactions comparable to those in question. In drawing on both data sources, the information processing required to complete the valuation of property is carried out through the sorting and search functions. Using these functions data can be sorted through any process of indexation and simple mathematical functions can be undertaken to analyse evidence of transactions, standard units of measurement and carry out the calculations required for the valuation of property. The calculation function requires particular attention. Here the holdings are classified in terms of the standard criteria set out by CIPFA and RICS.

The appraisal of land and buildings in the urban environment

The classification of holdings is made in terms of specialist, non-specialist assets held for operational purposes, investment, or surplus to requirements on the trading account. The standards of property valuation laid down in the RICS (1995) *Appraisal and Valuation Manual* are applied. This draws upon information contained in the property transactions file and the analysis of current values, construction costs and notional pricing mechanisms available for the valuation of property. Here again the data processing facilities can be applied to the valuation of property so as to provide notional prices for individual assets, or statements of asset value for groups, sectors, even geographical areas of the territory in question.

It is normally through this means the 'automated' valuation of property, for either individual or a 'mass' of assets is carried out. Such assessments tend to be carried out for groups of similar, or comparable subjects with the same classification, base and method for the valuation of commercial, industrial and housing categories of the property market and goes some way to provide the benchmarks to measure the performance of the holdings in question. Such benchmarks are drawn from the degree of usage, cost of outgoings, yield and level of rental growth. Together they represent standards of performance measurement that make it possible to compare assets forming the portfolio of holdings against property in general. This also provides the information to design a strategy towards the acquisition, utilisation, development and disposal of assets within the portfolio of holdings.

This is done by drawing on the results of the measurement and its ranking of performance as good, average or poor. If a subject ranks as average, or poor, the asset in question can be selected for review by either (operational/investment), holding (retail, office, industrial, residential) sector (prime, secondary) or area (within the centre, inner or outer suburbs) and subject to a rationalisation. As such a review and/or rationalisation is contingent upon the performance measurement, customised reports need to be specified for such programmes.

Turning to the question of how the computer-based information system designed to fulfil the three main management functions actually operates, it is perhaps best to demonstrate the practicalities of asset registration, property valuation and performance measurement by providing examples of the way it works to improve the standards of property management. To do this it is perhaps best to represent the computer-based information system as a register of asset classifications, set of, bases, methods of property valuation and performance measurement techniques, drawn upon by an 'expert' to model the appraisal process. Or as an expert system that provides a register of assets, valuation of property - be it through a form of an electronic filing cabinet, automated valuation of property and measurement of performance.

Figure 5.3, shows the asset register in terms of 'basic information', central committee, measurement, tenure (lease, rent details, review, termination pattern) market analysis and occupier. Figure 5.4 illustrates the type of information held on each asset for the valuation of property. Information, that is, on asset type, base and method of property valuation, category of holding, sector and techniques in terms of either rental, or capital transfer prices and yield drawn upon as part of the appraisal process.

Given the portfolio of asset classes the information system manages is heterogeneous in nature requiring; as it does: bases and methods of property valuation - not to mention performance measurement - suitable for the commercial, industrial and residential categories of holdings in the prime and secondary sectors, the full significance of the development tends to become apparent. Unlike previous studies which tend to focus on the valuation of either the commercial (predominantly office) or residential sectors of the property market, this form of appraisal (the registration of assets and valuation property) cannot rely on the conventions of the income approach, but must also supplement the comparative and investment methods with those of the contractors and residual. This is something that requires the adoption of asset classes and both the open market value (OMV) and depreciated replacement cost (DRC) as bases and methods for the valuation of property, measurement of performance and notional pricing of the holdings in question. The effect of this is to open up the traditional division in the methods of property valuation about the basis of the former to provide good reliable evidence of values and prices assets will exchange for in the market, rather than the more subjective valuation of what a property is worth as a holding under the latter. Given it has also been traditional for both the public and independent sector to hold a large amount of specialist assets for operational use relative to investment and development properties, the lack of opportunity to make use of the income approach and requirement to rely on cost, has tended to give a perception of the property management in such organisations as having only a distant relationship to the market. Indeed it is a view that has done much to reproduce the status quo in property management.

Basic Information

Use:
Description:
Street number:
Town/city: Name:
Ward: Postcode:
Account: OS Ref No:
Classifications:
Holding purpose (O/I/S to R):
Category (R, B, I* W & D, O*):
Acquisition date: Use class order:
Historic cost: Listed status:
Valuation basis (OMV/DRC):
Valuation: Rateable value:
Date of Valuation ( ):

Central Committee Data

Latest report:
Purpose:
Decision:

Measurement

Analysis (NIA/NEA/GIA/GEA):
Site (acres/hectares):
Floor area (sq.ft/ sq.metres):

Tenure

Ownership (F/L):
Title ref: Lease start date:
Lease ref: Termination date:
Rent roll ref: Frequency (Y/H/Q/M):
Current rent date: Passing rent:
Rent sq.ft/metre: Rent review pattern (yrs):

Market Analysis

Current value:
Market yield:

Occupier

User:
Owner:
Agents: Correspondence address:

....

Figure 5.3   Asset Register

File Reference:

Asset classification (S, N-S)
Base (OMV, DRC, AHC)
Method (C, I, R, C*, P)
Category (R, B, I, &, W&D, O*)
Market sector (P*, S*)
Technique
Direct capital comparison: All-risks yield:
Rack rented: Initial yield:
Term and revision: Reversionary yield:
Hardcore/layered: Equivalent yield:
Site Value: Equated yield:
Replacement cost:
Turnover:
Discounted cash flow:
Rational:
Real:

Figure 5.4   Property Valuation

Key to Figures 5.3 and 5.4:

O	=	Operational	M	=	Monthly
I	=	Investment	OMV	=	Open market value
S to R	=	Surplus to requirement	DRC	=	Depreciated replacement cost
P*	=	Prime	AHC	=	Amortised historic cost
S*	=	Secondary	C	=	Comparative
NIA	=	Net internal area	C*	=	Contractor's
NEA	=	Net external area	P	=	Profit
GIA	=	Gross internal areas	R	=	Retail
GEA	=	Gross external area	B	=	Business
F	=	Freehold	I	=	Industrial
L	=	Leasehold	W & D	=	Warehouse
Y	=	Yearly	O	=	Other
H	=	Half yearly	Q	=	Quarterly

This discussion shows that fundamental developments in the subject are taking place which tend to challenge such a view - the adoption of net current replacement as the principle of notional pricing, be it approached on the basis of income or cost - to mention but a few. Moreover, if it can be accepted the income approach concentrates on the investment method and in its present form only covers that category and sector of the market which generates income from standard, non-specialist property (predominantly in the independent sector), the extent of the developments taking place can be brought into focus. Put in as few words as possible, it is perhaps best seen as the development of an emergent pro-corporate, accountable, decentralised and competitive form of property valuation which cuts across the specialist, non-specialist, or standard classification and incorporates the logic of the income form in an attempt to price the full cost of management.

When this cannot be done through the application of the income approach (because the assets in question are non-standard, or specialist and not open to the investment method), it is done through the use of the cost approach on the basis of depreciated replacement and the contractor's method. For it is this form of property valuation that generates an income from specialist, non-standard holdings as a return on investment. Given the income it generates represent a rental payment in the form of a capital charge, the return it provides from the structure of yields in the market (to cover notional interest, obsolescence and depreciation) represents the price paid for the right to occupy the asset under a leasehold agreement and with the tenant responsible for the payment of outgoings.

But, perhaps most significant of all is the fact what such a development goes to demonstrate is that irrespective of whether the notional pricing exercise is of standard, non-specialist, or specialist assets, of any category, or sector, a form of investment method operates and is drawn upon as the basis of property valuation and performance measurement.

Under these circumstances, perhaps the most pertinent question to ask is what form of investment method and whether-or-not these subtle twists in the theory and method of property valuation bring about an equivalence, or uniform set of standards between the public and independent sector? To answer this question it is perhaps best to begin by looking more closely at the institutional setting of the development and listing the 'pros and cons' of one approach relative to another. That is of the income against the form of valuation which is emerging under the transition to property management.

The advocates of the income approach would no doubt want to stress that the emerging form of valuation tends to take the most appropriate elements of its own methodology and augments it with some kind of contractor-based 'capital asset pricing model', the value of which has already come under criticism from advocates of the income approach and pro-investment appraisal lobby - albeit in another, less radical form (see Baum 1989, 1991; Deakin, 2000a, 2000b). One whose rather crude treatment of the income-cost relationship, question of risk, growth, obsolescence and depreciation would no doubt attract considerable criticism for the simple fact it does not meet the 'market test'. Because, in essence, there is no evidence of any market transactions taking place on such a basis and due to the nature of the assets forming the subject of property valuation i.e. non-standard and specialist, there perhaps never will be - outside, that is, a more radical shake-up of finance, further re-organisation and reform, which at this point appears unlikely.

Table 5.3   The Income and Emerging Form

Pros	Income	Emerging form
	Relies on market evidence from analysis of transactions comparable in nature	Competitive, decentralist accountable and corporatist
	Bases the notional prices of property on the investment method of valuation	Bases its notional pricing on replacement cost, the valuation of standard, non-specialist and specialist assets in the commercial and industrial categories/sectors and adopts the investment and contractor's method of property valuation along with the comparative method for residential holdings
	Is growth, risk and depreciation explicit	The valuation of specialist assets adopts a contractor's form of asset pricing with a rate of return on investment from the structure of yields in the capital market
	Draws on independent evidence to compare the relationship between valuation and price	Makes use of independent standards of financial control over budgeting for audit, review, asset registration, property valuation and performance measurement whenever possible
Cons	Narrow focus on standard, non-specialist classification of assets and investment method of valuation	As yet the income it generates is not sensitive to risk, growth implicit and problematic in its treatment of obsolescence and depreciation
	Does not incorporate a large section of the 'market'	The landlord and tenant type relations of the internal market which underpin such a structure of income are ill-defined
	Concentrates on the investment method with some consideration of the residual method for development purposes	Legal constraints restrict the circulation of capital into all classifications of assets - be they specialist/non-specialist, the commercial, industrial, or residential categories
	Offers no solution to the problem of non-standard, specialist property and is ambivalent about the nature of the relationship between the public and independent sector	The limited circulation of capital and lack of transactional data in the specialist sector make it difficult to obtain independent evidence of the relationship between valuations and price

While it would be correct to suggest much work needs to be done on the question of equivalence before it can be given any serious consideration, the outcome of taking such a stance on the matter is unfortunate in that it tends to undermine the value of such an investigation by imposing the standards of the income approach on the one in question. Rather than simply reproducing the status quo, it might perhaps be best to look at the matter as one which places both forms of property valuation under question and represents a position where no particular set of standards should be seen to dominate the other.

Looking at the matter in this way, it might be possible to hold on to the possibility of braking the strangle-hold the income approach has over property valuation and opening it up to contemporary developments of the kind outlined under this heading. But this is only half the story, for the development of the computer-based information systems outlined here also marks a radical break with more traditional forms of appraisal. This is because the computer-based information system outlined here not only draws upon the strategies, culture or communicative structure of property management, but the new model of service provision underlying the cutting and reshaping of expenditure this produces as part of the on-going re-organisation and reform. As such it mirrors the expertise of the user (be it the executive, directorate or experts within the property management division i.e. chief executives, finance, legal, estates sections etc.) to provide the information needed to carry out such functions.

The supply of information, which in this instance, is for the strategic management of property. The strategic management of property upon which the communicative structure rests and the said re-organisation and reform depend. As, what is in effect, the basis for such a 'high-tech, informational rich, economic cum cultural paradigm' of property management, the development can perhaps best be referred to as an expert system for the corporatisation, financial instruments and commercial standards (communicative structure) the management of property needs under the re-organisation (new model of service provision) and reform (the cutting and reshaping of expenditure) in question.

Conclusions

This paper has sought to examine the issues that underlie the development of computer-based information systems for the management of property. As such it has set out the issues that surround the application of IT to the development in question and has suggested the problems and difficulties currently being experienced in the application of IT, development of computer-based information systems and management of property, lie in the structure of local authority property management and both the theory and method of property management put forward by independent bodies like the AC and CIPFA.

While it is appreciated that bodies of this kind do not wish to be over-prescriptive in the form of property management they should like to see develop, it is evident the translation of the theory which focuses attention on a competitive, decentred, accountable and corporate form of property management into a method of application (i.e. into a strategy geared towards the adoption of IT and development of computer-based information systems) requires a great deal of further consideration if the exercise is to produce something more valuable than an electronic filing cabinet. If, that is, it is going to improve the standards of property management by progressing through this preliminary stage of development and do so in the manner which allows the valuation of property and measurement of performance to take place.

The paper has documented how such a transition from electronic filing cabinet to automated property valuation and performance measurement is being achieved. It has also drawn attention to how the application of IT and development of such an information system aids the appraisal of land and buildings in the urban environment. In this respect it has sought to show how the development in question represents an emergent form of property valuation which challenges the conventions of the income approach as part of an attempt to cut across the asset classes, bases and methods of property valuation in an attempt to price the full cost of holding land and buildings. In doing so it has drawn attention to the radical nature of the break this emerging form of property valuation makes with more established conventions. In view of this, it has also sought to qualify the significance of the development and balance the 'pros and cons' of the conventional position against the more radical nature of the emergent form. While such a representation tends to emphasise the somewhat radical nature of the development, it is important not to mis-represent the situation as a straightforward innovation in the valuation of property, for this should be wrong and would run the considerable risk of trivialising a matter of even greater concern. On the contrary, the development should be seen as anything but a straightforward innovation in the valuation of property and ought to be seen as a response to the overall restructuring of property management currently taking place.

Chapter 6

Sustainable Urban Development: the Framework and Directory of Assessment Methods

Introduction

This chapter documents the interim findings of the BEQUEST (Building Environmental Quality Evaluation for Sustainability) network and the project's investigation of sustainable urban development. The network has its origins in an international conference: 'The Environmental Impact of Buildings and Cities', held in Florence in 1995 (Brandon, et al 1997). More recently the network has been funded by the Research Directorate of the EU Framework 4 Programme. The project sets out to develop a common language and approach to Sustainable Urban Development (SUD) and aims to produce a framework, directory of assessment methods and set of procurement protocols for such purposes. The framework, assessment methods and procurement protocols, are currently in the process of being linked together in the form of a tool-kit. It is anticipated this instrument will be of particular use for those advising on the sustainability of urban development and taking decisions about the city of tomorrow and its cultural heritage.

The EU Environment and Climate Programme

Although BEQUEST is a Framework 4 project, it addresses Action 4: City of Tomorrow and Cultural Heritage of the EU Environment and Climate Programme in Framework 5. The aims and objectives of BEQUEST relate to Section 4.1 of the City of Tomorrow and Cultural Heritage. It is also relevant to Section 4.3 and the paragraphs referring to sustainable development, resource conservation and environmental protection in particular. In terms of the EU's document: 'Sustainable Urban Development: A Framework for Action' (CEU 1998), the project also raises awareness of SUD, by exploring ways of utilising communication and information technology to exchange experiences in framing the relevant issues and assessing the effect resource conservation and environmental protection has upon the city of tomorrow and its cultural heritage.

The BEQUEST concerted action

The BEQUEST concerted action project aims to lay the foundations for a common understanding of sustainable urban development through a multi-disciplinary network of contributions from the scientific and professional communities. The research method adopted provides a structured process of interaction between the wide range of interests involved in the process of urban development (i.e. the planning, provision, use and maintenance of the built environment as a form of human settlement). Mature deliberation, debate and evolution are key elements of the project and develop through an iterative learning cycle of workshops, reflection and concerted action. The project partners, known as the Intranet, act as the mentors and facilitators of this process. Extranet members participate in the project though the workshops and by means of follow-up comments on information papers. Using communication systems, including a web page, the workshops provide the project partners and extranet members with the information technology needed for the networked community to debate SUD and enter into a dialogue about resource conservation and environmental protection. Together the intranet and extranet represent the type of community needed to **B**uild **E**nvironmental capacity, **QU**alify whether the city of tomorrow is able to carry its cultural heritage and **E**valuate if the forms of human settlement resulting from this process of urban development are su**ST**ainable. There are 14 partners in the BEQUEST EU project and over 130 extranet members in the networked community. To date seven international workshops have been held (Milton Keynes, Amsterdam, Turin, Helsinki, Florence, Vienna and Lisbon) and further details of this work, together with the associated information papers can be found at the following web-site address: http://www.surveying.salford.ac.uk/bq/extra. The web site also provides an outline of the project, the partners and extranet members. What follows reports on the interim findings of work carried out on two of the project objectives: the framework for a common understanding of sustainable development and directory of assessment methods.

A framework for a common understanding

As any standard textbook on environmental issues points out, what sustainable development means is difficult to define. The first commonly accepted meaning of the term was that offered by the Brundtland Report, which defines it as:

> development that meets the needs of the present without compromising the ability of future generations to meet their own needs (WCED, 1987:43).

Subsequently the U.N. 'Earth Summit', held in Rio in 1992, developed a wider concept known as Agenda 21 and represented in shorthand form as Figure 6.1 (Mitchell et al 1995, as developed by Cooper, 1997). This focuses on a four-sided definition of sustainable development. Here attention is drawn to the concern about the quality of the environment, the equity of resource consumption, as well as the participation of the public in decisions taken about the future of the urban development process. It is this four-fold (environment, equity, participation and futurity) representation of sustainable development that the BEQUEST project has adopted. Following the discussion of 'human settlement' appearing in the Brundtland Report, Agenda 21 and the UN Habitat Conference in 1996, the project has sought to draw upon these definitions as a means of moving the EU towards a framework for a common understanding of sustainable development.

In Europe, human settlement is pre-dominantly urban in form (2/3 of EU citizens live in towns or cities) and as a consequence, questions about sustainable development relate to matters concerning the future of this particular development process. In particular they are matters that relate to questions about the development of urban futures, cities of tomorrow and their cultural heritage. They are questions about how to build the capacity needed to not only conserve resources and protect the environment, but qualify and evaluate whether such action is equitable and dealt with in a manner which fosters public participation in decisions taken about the future of urban development.

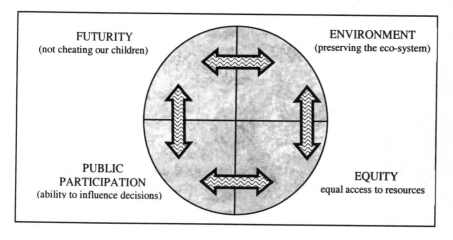

Figure 6.1   The Fourfold Definition of Sustainable Development

Source: Adapted from Cooper (1997)

Fore-grounding the urban question

The project has sought to identify the common issues underlying this growing interest in sustainable development and structure them in such a way as to provide a framework for analysis (Nijkamp, 1991; Mitchell, et al, 1995; Haughton and Hunter, 1994; Miltin and Satterhwaite, 1996; Pugh, 1996; Mazza and Rydin, 1997). This has been done by first adopting the Mitchell, et al (1995) definition of sustainable development, 'mapping out' the 'fuzzy buzzwords' (Palmer, et al, 1997) associated with the concept and by then modifying it to include the issues underlying the urban process. The Mitchell, et al (1995) model of sustainable development provides the opportunity to 'map out' the multitude of meanings - 'the buzzwords' - and agree on what they all have in common. This has led to the project developing a common language to communicate what is meant by SUD and agree the vocabulary to be used in addressing the subject. The agreed vocabulary takes the form of a 'glossary', setting out the terminology to be employed in addressing the issues in question. This in turn provides the terms of reference needed to 'frame' the relevant issues (structure them in space and time) and direct decision makers towards the technology currently available to assess the sustainability of urban development. This modification has required the following:

- fore-grounding the question of urban development (Nijkamp, 1991) and representing the process of urbanisation as a life cycle of inter-related activities;
- agreeing the sustainable development issues (Miltin and Satterhwaite, 1996) underlying the urban process;
- identifying the environmental, economic and social structure, spatial level and time scales of sustainable urban development (Pugh, 1996).

In fore-grounding the urban question, the project has sub-divided the development process by division of labour in the scientific and professional communities. The division of labour is question is that of urban development: planning, design, construction and operation (use, demolition and recycling). Representing the process of urbanisation as a life cycle of inter-related activities, the sustainable development issues that surface concern the environmental, economic and social structure, spatial level and time scales of SUD. The spatial level of analysis identifies the territorial impact of urban development. This illustrates that the impact can be at the city, district, neighbourhood, estate, building, component and material level. The consideration of time-scales also shows that the said impact can be short, medium and long-term in nature.

Towards a directory of environmental assessment methods

While the aforesaid provides a framework for analysis, it does not address the question of how decision makers can reverse the current trend of resource depletion, conserve resources and protect the environment? That is build the environmental capacity needed to ensure the city of tomorrow is able to carry its cultural heritage and develop forms of human settlement which are sustainable. To achieve this it is necessary to: a) qualify whether the capacity exists for the city of tomorrow to carry its cultural heritage and b) evaluate if the forms of human settlement which surface from this process of urban development are sustainable.

In addressing these questions, the network has agreed the sustainable development issues underlying the process of urbanisation. These have been defined in terms of the environmental, economic, social and institutional issues underlying the urban development process. Here environmental issues take on the form of considerations about how the process of urbanisation consumes natural resources, whether it produces emissions that pollute the atmosphere and the effect development has upon the bio-diversity of habitats. Economic considerations relate to questions about the financing of the infrastructures, transport and utilities required for the built environment to accommodate the urban development process and employment of resources associated with this. The social issues concern matters about access to such services, the safety and security of cities, human health and well-being cultural heritage provides (see Figure 6.2). The institutional issues refer to the governance, justice and ethics of settlement patterns subject to urban development.

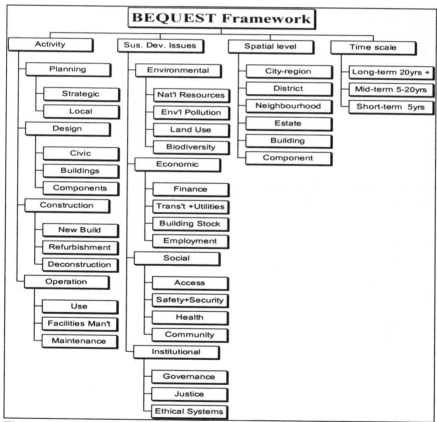

Figure 6.2   The BEQUEST Framework

The reason why sustainable development issues, their spatial levels and time scales raise questions about environmental assessment is of particular significance. This is because many of the assessment methods currently in existence are pre-Brundtland and in their present form do not adequately address the questions of resource conservation, environmental protection, or sustainable development (Pearce and Markauya, 1989; Pearce and Turner, 1990; Norgaard and Howarth, 1991). Many of the assessment methods currently in existence can be traced back to cost benefit analysis and the critique of the discounting principle this technique of analysis is based upon (Rydin, 1992; Deakin, 1996, 1997, 1999). Their development can also be linked to the emergence of hedonic and non-market techniques of analysis as alternative forms of assessment. Techniques of analysis such as the contingent value and travel cost methods of environmental assessment (Miltin and Satterhwaite, 1996; Brooks, et al, 1997; Powell, et al, 1997). Since the Brundtland Report, environmental assessment has been placed under investigation by the green movement and critical distinctions have been drawn between eco and anthropocentric techniques of analysis (Pearce and Warford, 1993). Since the Rio Earth Summit, attention has also turned to the concept of 'ecological footprint' and use of it as a means to qualify whether the environmental capacity exists for the city of tomorrow to carry its cultural heritage (Rees, 1992; Kozlowski and Hill, 1993; Breheny 1992a, 1992b; 1995; Breheny and Rookwood 1993; Breheny, et al, 1993; Selman, 1996). In turn attention has subsequently focussed on evaluating if the forms of human settlement surfacing from this process of urban development are sustainable (Brandon, et al, 1997).

Recent surveys of environmental assessment

Recent surveys of environmental assessment examine how the methods are currently being used. The examinations in question provide:

- reviews of how assessment methods are being drawn upon to promote sustainable development through resource conservation and environmental protection policies (Therivel, 1992; Glasson, et al, 1994; Jowsey and Kellnet, 1996; Lichfield, 1996);
- evaluations of the impact major infrastructure and building installation projects have upon resource conservation, environmental protection and the sustainable development of cities (Guy and Marvin, 1997; Marvin and Guy, 1997; Brandon, et al, 1997);
- meta-analysis' of the potential that assessment methods have to conserve resources, build environmental capacity and ensure the city of tomorrow is able to carry its cultural heritage in forms of human settlement which are sustainable (Bergh, et al, 1997; Nijkamp and Pepping, 1998).

Such surveys illustrate the gaps that exist between the inter-related activities of the urban life cycle the assessment methods cover and the sustainable development issues which the techniques of analysis address (Cooper, 1997). An example of this can be found in the different assessment techniques used in the EIA of larger urban development projects (i.e. infrastructure design proposals) and those drawn upon to assess individual building installations (Cooper and Curwell, 1998). The surveys also reveal that scientific opinion about the potential of environmental assessment is currently divided. Firstly, there are those who are of the opinion environmental assessment methods can be used to promote sustainable development (Brandon, et al, 1997; Bergh, 1997; Nijkamp and Pepping, 1998). Secondly, there are others who are of the opinion the all-pervasive marketisation, privatisation of the environment and resultant risk and uncertainty surrounding the nature of public goods, means the methods currently available are no longer appropriate. As a consequence, they tend to question whether we have the appropriate methods for the assessment of SUD (Guy and Marvin, 1997a). This division of opinion is important for two reasons. Firstly, because it illustrates the scientific community is divided about the value of assessment methods. Secondly, the division of opinion tends to undermine the certainty the professional community needs in order to be confident about the worth of such assessments (Pugh, 1996; Cooper, 1997, 99).

The position adopted by the network

The position the network has taken on the matter tends to align with the first opinion. This is because the network is of the view that the environmental assessment methods can be used to promote sustainable urban development and the uncertainty and risk which surrounds the process of privatisation represents a particular, but not insurmountable challenge for the scientific community. The network is of the opinion that the source of such division lies in the absence of appropriate frameworks and the less than systematic approach that has previously been taken towards the inter-related activities of the urban life cycle, sustainable development issues, spatial levels and time scales drawn attention to (Curwell et al, 1998; Cooper and Curwell, 1998).

The assessment methodology the project adopts is based upon an understanding that the growing international and increasingly global nature of the relationship between the environment and economy is uncertain, resulting in as yet incalculable degrees of risk associated with EC policy and any actions which member states take on resource conservation. This in turn means that standard methods of environmental valuation are of limited help in building the capacity needed to qualify whether the city of tomorrow is able to carry its cultural heritage and if the forms of human settlement which develop from this process of urban development are sustainable. This is because such assessments increasingly require the use of non-standard valuation (hedonic and contingency type) methods (Powell, et al 1997).

Perhaps more critically, though, the network is of the opinion that methods of this kind are of limited use in assessing sustainable development and it is necessary to transcend such valuations as part of a co-evolutionary approach to environmental assessment. This is an approach that uses a holistic framework for the analysis of sustainable development and represents the environmental, economic and social as complementary (Facheaux et al, 1996; O'Conner, 1998; Facheaux and O'Conner, 1998). Complementary in the sense that resource conservation reduces depletion rates, protects the environment and builds the capacity the city of tomorrow has to carry its cultural heritage. The environmental capacity - it should be added - the city of tomorrow needs to carry its cultural heritage in economic and social structures that in turn develop forms of human settlement which are sustainable. Forms of human settlement that are sustainable in terms of the quality of life they in turn institute. It should perhaps also be noted that this concern with the quality of life is significant because it transcends the issues which are of current concern to environmental valuation (property rights, landscape, recreation and leisure), shifts attention to valuing the environment in terms of ecosystem integrity (resource consumption, pollution, land use and bio-diversity) and the scientific basis of such assessments.

Transcending environmental valuation

What such assessments do is turn attention towards the ecology of resource consumption. The advantage of this lies in the opportunity that assessments of this kind provide to develop methods which apply the so-called 'hard' certainties of bio-physical science to the more uncertain, risky social relations. The relations that are 'softer' and which are by nature more difficult to predict (Facheaux and O'Conner, 1998). This is done by emphasising the co-evolutionary nature of the bio-physical and social in a framework for analysis that integrates the environmental, economic and social and which in turn provides the methodology for assessing the sustainability of development. What this does is focus attention on the hard and soft issues of sustainable development (Fusco, et al, 1997; Capello, et al, 1999). The issues that in this instance are integrated in the form of the environmental appraisal, supported by economic and social impact analyses which provide statements about the sustainability of development. Environmental appraisals and impact analyses that transcend existing valuation techniques and which in turn develop as forms of sustainability assessments.

Transforming environmental assessment

What is significant about such methods is the tendency they illustrate to not only transcend existing valuation techniques, but also transform environmental assessment per se. This is because as forms of sustainability assessments, such methods (i.e. environmental appraisals and impact analyses) not only transcend existing valuation techniques, but also go a long way to transform environmental assessment methodology. What such methods do is to transform into a post-Brundtland directory of environmental assessment methods. Into the directory of environmental assessment methods needed to a) qualify whether the capacity exists for the city of tomorrow to carry its cultural heritage and b) evaluate if the economic and social structures that underlie this process of urban development produce forms of human settlement which are sustainable.

The post-Brundtland directory

In response to this, members of the network have sought to survey the methods currently in existence and provide a post-Brundtland directory of environmental assessment. The methods surveyed are classified in terms of the following:

- name
- description
- data required
- status (well established, or experimental)
- activity (planning, design, construction and operation)
- environmental and social issues (environmental, economic, social and institutional)
- scale of assessment (spatial level and time scale)
- references

So far, the survey has identified that 64 such methods are available to conserve resources and build environmental capacity. It has also identified the said methods have been applied to the planning, design, construction and operational activities of the urban life cycle and used to analyse the sustainability issues this raises at the various levels scales of assessment.

The directory can be accessed at the web-site address previously referred to. The website provides a copy of each standard classification and in a number of cases offers hypertext links to the case studies they have been drawn from. This provides the opportunity for the reader to explore the implications of applying the method in further detail and satisfying themselves as to whether the technique is appropriate for the assessment under consideration. The list of methods is drawn from a survey of the scientific literature and unpublished reports written by professional members of the community. In certain cases they represent assessment methods the partner and extranet members of the network have been engaged in developing or have a detailed knowledge of. A full list of the environmental assessment methods can be found in Appendix: List of Environmental Assessment Methods.

The assessment methods

The assessment methods fall into two classes: 'environmental valuations' and those developing into particular forms of 'sustainability assessments'. The survey has found that post-Brundtland, environmental valuations tend to focus on assessments of eco-system integrity. It has also been found that those methods developing into particular forms of sustainability assessments, tend to focus on building the environmental capacity needed to not only qualify the integrity of eco-systems, but evaluate the equity, participation and futurity of the economic, social and institutional structures underlying the city of tomorrow, its cultural heritage and forms of human settlement.

Table 6.1   Environmental Assessment Methods

Environmental Valuations	Forms of Sustainability Assessment	
	Environmental Appraisal	EIA
Contingent Valuation Cost benefit analysis Hedonic analysis Multi-criteria analysis Travel cost theory	Compatibility matrix Eco-profiling Ecological footprint Environmental auditing Flag method Spider analysis	Project Strategic • economic • social Community evaluation BEES BREEAM Eco-points Green Building Code MASTER Framework Meta-analysis (Pentagon method) NAR model Quantitative city model Regime analysis SPARTACUS Sustainable City model Sustain. communities Sustainable regions Transit-oriented settlement

Source: See Appendix

Examples of the 'environmental valuation' class of methods include: cost-benefit analysis, hedonic analysis and multi-criteria analysis. The forms of sustainability assessments have been sub-classified as 'environmental appraisal' (simple base-line qualifications) and 'environmental impact assessments' (complex and advanced evaluations). They include: the compatibility matrix, eco-profiling and environmental auditing (environmental appraisal). The environmental impact assessments (EIA's) include: project, strategic, economic, social and community evaluations (complex), BEES, BREEAM, Eco-points and the Green Building Code. It also includes, the MASTER Framework, the Pentagon model, the Quantitative City model, SPARTACUS, the sustainable city model, sustainable community, sustainable region and the Transit-orientated settlement model, as advanced forms of environmental assessment. Examples of these two classifications are set out in Table 6.1.

In terms of the environmental valuations and forms of sustainability assessments, the methods tend to further sub-divide into the following types:

- methods supporting the post-Brundtland commitment to sustainable development in terms of the policies adopted by the EU and its member states (Bentivenga, 1997; Davoudi, 1997; Therivel, 1998);
- those centring on the assessments of projects providing the infrastructures (energy, water and drainage, transport, tele-communication technologies, leisure and tourism) required to build the environmental capacity needed for the city of tomorrow to carry its cultural heritage (Banister and Burton, 1993; Nijkamp and Pepping, 1994; Graham and Marvin, 1996; Nijkamp, et al, 1997; Guy and Marvin, 1997a, b; Jones, et al, 1996; Allwinkle and Speed, 1997);
- those assessment methods that focus on the procurement of construction and installation of operations for the purposes of forming human settlement which are sustainable (Prior, 1993; Vale and Vale, 1993; Cole, 1997; Curwell, et al, 1999; Deakin, 1999).

Building environmental capacity

The survey of the assessment methods currently being used to conserve resources and build environmental capacity is drawn from those assessment methods listed in Appendix. It represents the classification of each method by inter-related activities of the urban life cycle. The sustainable development issues, spatial level and time scale that both classes of assessment methods (environment valuations and forms of sustainability assessments) are applied to with the object of building environmental capacity.

Figure 6.3 maps the methods by the inter-related activities (planning, design, construction and operation) of the urban life cycle, sustainable development issues, spatial level and time scale of assessment. It illustrates the strength of representation spread across the range of activities making up the aforesaid. In this aggregated form, the survey provides evidence to suggest a wide range of methods exist to assess the environmental capacity of all the activities (planning, design, construction and operational activities) making up the urban life cycle, sustainable development issues, spatial level and time scales.

		Planning	Design	Construction	Operation
Sustainable Development Issues	Environmental				
	Economic				
	Social				
	Institutional				
Spatial Level	City-region				
	District				
	Neighbourhood				
	Estate				
	Building				
	Component				
Time Scales	Long				
	Medium				
	Short				
		Policy			
		Infrastructure			
		Procurement			
		Installation			

Figure 6.3   Assessment Methods

Source: Mapping of Appendix

Note: the shading is indicative of the 'intensity scores', or 'frequency' by which the assessment methods address the sustainable urban development issues in question. The shadings score the frequency by which the assessment methods' address the issues in terms of high, medium, low and no representation. The five degrees of shading roughly approximate to 75-100 per cent, 50 -75 per cent, 25-50 per cent and O per cent representation of the issues at the specified spatial level and time scales.

The purpose of mapping the assessment methods by such co-ordinates is fourfold. First, it illustrates the range and spread of methods currently available. Secondly, it provides the means by which to identify how the assessment methods are being used. Thirdly, it identifies the strength of representation by SUD, spatial level and time scale. Fourthly, it draws attention to the gaps that exist in the range and spread of methods needed to assess the sustainability of urban development. It also provides the opportunity to direct further research aimed at developing the methodology (science, theory and practice) of environmental assessment.

What the mapping exercise suggests is that the scientific and professional communities are drawing on assessment methods to build environmental capacity. It provides evidence to suggest the assessment methods are being used to build environmental capacity in the policy planning, infrastructure design, construction procurement activities and those associated with operation of installations. It also illustrates that it is the urban life cycle, sustainable development issues, spatial levels and time scales of the planning policy and infrastructure design activities, which are the most strongly represented forms of assessment. This is because the other forms of assessment (construction and operation) are not as well covered in terms of sustainable development issues, spatial level, or time scale (see Figure 6.3). This suggest that the gaps which exist in the range and spread of methods needed to provide a integrated assessment are located here in the construction and operation stages of the urban life cycle, their particular sustainable development issues, spatial levels and time scales.

It should be noted that Figure 6.3 does not map how the assessment methods represent the ecological integrity, equity, participation and futurity issues underlying the sustainability issues of the urban development process. To be explicit about this further analysis will need to be carried out. This will need to extend the analysis beyond the matrix-based mapping set out in Figure 6.3 and introduce a more comprehensive grid referencing system. One that can map, not only the urban development process in terms of its life cycle, sustainability, spatial levels and time scale, but cross-reference them with the ecological integrity, equity, participation and futurity components of the assessment methods in a form of 'frontier analysis'.

What follows will limit its observations to the mapping exercise of Figure 6.3 and set out what it tells us about the attempts being made to build environmental capacity. This will include references to how environmental assessment methods are currently being used to qualify whether the city of tomorrow has the capacity that is needed to carry its cultural heritage and evaluate if the forms of human settlement which surface from this process of urban development are sustainable.

The qualifications and evaluations

It is proposed that Figure 6.3 provides evidence to suggest:

1. A number of methods exist to assess the post-Brundtland commitment towards sustainable development and these include:

    -   CBA, contingent valuation, travel cost, hedonic and multi-criteria analysis, to assess the environmental value of urban development proposals;
    -   simple base-line methods drawn upon to assess the integrity of eco-systems and ensure the economic, social and institutional issues underlying the process of urbanisation are consistent with policy commitments towards sustainable development. Examples of such methods appear under the title of 'environmental appraisal' and include: the compatibility matrix, eco-profiling and environmental auditing techniques;

- the use of more complex methods to assess whether infrastructure projects (servicing energy, water and drainage, transport, telecommunication technologies, leisure and tourism services), build the environmental capacity that is needed for the city of tomorrow to carry its cultural heritage in forms of human settlement which are economically efficient in the way they accommodate growth, encourage competitiveness and the social cohesion of institutions. Examples of such methods appear under the heading of EIA and include project, strategic, economic, social and community evaluations;
- the development of complex methods that assess the environmental capacity of operational installations and evaluate whether the forms of human settlement which it provides are sustainable in these terms. These evaluations include BREEAM, Eco-points, the Green Building Code, the net annual return (NAR) model of EIA;
- the emergence of advanced methods which assess (at the level of policy and infrastructure projects) the ecological integrity and equity of alternative urban development paths. The alternative urban development paths it is possible for the public to participate in selecting. Participate in the selection of and chose as those 'futures' best able to build the environmental capacity that is needed for the city of tomorrow to carry its cultural heritage in forms of human settlement which is sustainable. These methods include the MASTER Framework, the Pentagon model, the Quantitative City model, SPARTACUS, the Sustainable City, sustainable region, sustainable communities and Transit-orientated settlement models.

2. The methods are used in a specific or more general capacity. That is as a means to assess the environmental capacity of a specific stage in the urban development process i.e. qualifying if the planning policy associated with the city of tomorrow has the capacity to carry its cultural heritage, or for the more general purpose of evaluating if the design and construction activities connected with the operation of installations produce forms of human settlement which are sustainable (Birtles, 1997; Cooper, 1997, 1999). Here it is noticeable that environmental appraisals (in their simple, base-line forms) are used to quality whether the city of tomorrow has the capacity to carry its cultural heritage. It is also evident that it is the EIA's (as more complex and advanced assessments) which are used to evaluate if the forms of human settlement produced by the urban development process are sustainable. This indicates that it is the environmental appraisals undertaken to meet the statutory requirements of development planning which are being used to qualify whether the city of tomorrow has the capacity to carry its cultural heritage. This also suggests it is the EIA's that are being used to evaluate if the infrastructure designs and construction procurement activities of the operational stages produce forms of human settlement which are sustainable.

3. The use of the methods illustrates the growing inter-disciplinary nature of the assessment exercise, providing evidence of assessment methods being used to assess the following:

    -   the policy planning and infrastructure design of the urban development process;
    -   the infrastructure design, construction procurement and operational activities making up the city of tomorrow, its cultural heritage and forms of human settlement.

Irrespective of whether the methods in question are applied to policy planning, infrastructure design, construction procurement, or the installation of operations, the object of the 'environment valuation' class is to assess the capacity (in this instance ecological integrity) of the sustainable development issues under consideration. With the application of this class, it is also noticeable that any economic analysis is confined to the planning and design stage of policy and infrastructure provision and does not extend into activities associated with either the construction, or operational stages. This is also the case for any social issues that surface from the application of such assessment methods. Perhaps most noticeable is the relative absence of any institutional analysis at this level of assessment.

With the 'forms of sustainability assessment' the situation is somewhat different. This is because with this class of method there is evidence to suggest the assessments take environmental capacity to include the equity, public participation and futurity of the sustainable development issues underlying the economic and social structures in question. It is also noticeable that in developing into this kind of assessment, it is common to see methods from the other classification (environmental valuations) embedded in and providing the environmental and economic foundation for the range of appraisals, economic and social impact assessments (forms of sustainability assessments) undertaken. This is common irrespective of whether the environmental appraisal and EIA is of the simple, complex, or even advanced type. Examples of this occur with the use of CBA in environmental appraisal and impact assessment (Glasson, et al, 1994; Lichfield, 1996; Therivel, 1998). It is also evident in the use of the multiple-regression component of the hedonic technique forming the meta-analysis of sustainability assessment (Berg, et al, 1997; Nijkamp, 1998). Another example of this can be found in the transformation of multi-criteria assessments into regime analysis and use of this to resolve environmental conflicts over the economic and social structure of sustainable development (Bizarro and Nijkamp, 1997). Although, even here, there is clear evidence to show the methods experience noticeable difficulties in dealing with the complexity of institutional structures and the range of stakeholder interests this introduces into any such assessment (Lombardi, 2001).

It is also common to see this transcendence of environmental valuation mediated through other assessment methods. Methods that take on the function of mechanisms which support the transformation of environmental assessment as part of the search for sustainable development. This is evident in the use of the analytical hierarchy process to transform MCA into the flag method and impact assessments undertaken as part of a regime analysis. It is also seen in the use of life cycle analysis to transform CBA into the NAR model of EIA. The model of environmental impact also adopted for the assessment of sustainable communities.

Another distinction that can be drawn from this transformation of environmental assessment relates to the way in which the hard and soft issues of sustainable development form part of the methodology. With certain forms of sustainability assessments: for example; BEES and the Quantifiable city model, the bio-physical forms the focus of attention. Here the sustainable development issues under assessment are those of energy consumption, material flows, waste and pollution. This is also the case for the Quantifiable city model. While valuable for focusing attention on the environment (in this sense ecological integrity), it should perhaps be noted that such methods do not integrate either the economic or social structures of the urban development process to the same degree as other forms of sustainability assessment. Methods that manage to balance the bio-physical and social and provide a more integrated environmental, economic and social assessment (of ecological integrity, equity, participation and futurity) include BREEAM, the MASTER Framework, SPARTACUS, the sustainable community, city, region and Transit-orientated settlement models.

4. The methods are being applied at different spatial levels of analysis and evidence exists to suggest these are as follows:

   - methods to assess the policy and planning of sustainable development are applied at the city-regional, district and neighbourhood levels of analysis;
   - these levels of analysis are also typical of the methods adopted to assess the policy planning and design of major infrastructure projects;
   - in terms of methods assessing the design, construction and operation of various installations, the levels of analysis adopted to evaluate whether the city of tomorrow has the capacity to carry its cultural heritage, tend to be those of the estate, building, component and material.

5. The time-scale implied in the assessment of policy commitment and both the planning and design of major infrastructure projects at the city-regional, district and neighbourhood scale, is medium to long term. However, often the political pressures for rapid reversal of areas in environmental stress, economic decline and social depravation, means that the opposite is the case. So, as with the design, construction and operation of the various building installations, short-term considerations can apply (Curwell and Lombardi, 1999).

6. The simple base-line and more complex methods tend to restrict the spatial level of assessment to the city-region, district, neighbourhood, estate, building and component level of analysis, while the advanced methods assess the

cumulative national, growing international and global impact of the urban development process over the long, medium and short term. In taking this form, the advanced assessment methods recognise the need for a pan-European understanding of the urban development process. This in turn recognises the need to develop assessment methods that are urban in nature. That is urban in the sense they provide the technologies and communicative structures required by member states to conserve resources and build the environmental capacity needed for the city of tomorrow to carry its cultural heritage. Furthermore, do so in a form of human settlement that are sustainable at diverse (i.e. macro, meso and microscopic) levels and scales of analysis (Brandon and Lombardi, 2001).

7.   While this suggests a great deal of headway has been made post-Brundtland to progress the theory, science and practice of assessment, it should be recognised that it is only the simple base-line methods which are currently well established. This is because the more advanced assessment methods are still experimental.

8.   It should also be recognised the following tend to restrict the degree of progress made in advancing the theory and practice of environmental assessment:

   •   the tendency for the policy planning and infrastructure design stages to overshadow the assessment needs of construction procurement and the operational stages of the urban development process (Cooper, 1997, 1999, 2000; Deakin, 2000, 2001);
   •   the paucity of environmental, economic and social (sustainable development) indicators it is possible to draw upon as a means of benchmarking the effect policy planning, infrastructure design, construction procurement and operation of various building installations has upon environmental capacity (Mitchell, 1996; 2000);
   •   the fact that this in turn makes it difficult - in methodological terms - to assess the aggregate effect the aforesaid have upon attempts to not only build environmental capacity, but use this as a means to qualify and evaluate the sustainability of urban development. Qualify if and evaluate whether, that is, the said development leads to the city of tomorrow having a cultural heritage and form of human settlement which is sustainable (Brandon and Lombardi, 2000; Cooper, 2000; Lombardi, 2000).

The aforesaid are restrictive because they tend to highlight the rather limited nature of the data-sets currently available to assess the sustainability of the urban development and inform us about the effect attempts to build environmental capacity have upon the city of tomorrow, its cultural heritage and forms of human settlement.

Conclusions

This chapter has outlined the areas of the Environment and Climate Programme (Economic and Social Aspects of Human Settlement) the BEQUEST project addresses, examined the framework it sets out for a common understanding of sustainable development and assessment methods currently made use of by planners, architects, engineers and surveyors to build environmental capacity. It has gone on to set out the issues the project addresses in transcending environmental valuations, transforming assessment methodology and moving towards a post-Brundtland directory of environmental assessment methods. This in turn has led to a classification of the environmental assessment methods contained in the directory.

The paper has established that the methods in question fall into two classes: 'environmental valuations' and those which develop into forms of 'sustainability assessments'. It has shown the environment valuations tend to focus on assessments of eco-system integrity. It has also illustrated that those methods augmenting into particular forms of sustainability assessment, tend to focus on building the environmental capacity which is needed to not only ensure the integrity of eco-systems, but the equity, participation and futurity (sustainability) of the economic, social and institutional structures underlying the urban development process. The examination has highlighted some of the problems currently associated with the application of the environmental assessment methods. This has drawn attention to a number of weaknesses in how the methods qualify whether the city of tomorrow has the capacity to carry its cultural heritage and evaluate if the forms of human settlement which surface from this process of urban development are sustainable. This in turn has drawn particular attention to the need for further research aimed at:

- extending the analysis beyond the matrix-based mapping set out in this paper and introducing a more comprehensive grid referencing system. One that can map, not only the urban development process in terms of its life cycle, sustainability, spatial levels and temporal scale, but cross-reference them with the ecological integrity, equity, participation and futurity components of the assessment in a form of 'frontier analysis';
- addressing the difficulties current assessment methods have in dealing with the complexity of institutional structures and associated stakeholder interests;
- overcoming the tendency for the policy planning and infrastructure design stages of the urban development process, to overshadow the assessment needs of other activities and result in a situation whereby comparatively speaking, relatively little is known about either the procurement of construction, or installation of operations;
- augmenting the sustainable development indicators it is possible to draw upon as a means of measuring the effect planning policy, infrastructure design, construction procurement and activities associated with the operation of building installations has upon environmental capacity;

- developing the means to assess the aggregate effect of the aforesaid upon attempts to build environmental capacity and in turn qualify not only whether the city of tomorrow is able to carry its cultural heritage, but evaluate if the forms of human settlement which surface from this process of urban development are sustainable.

Finally, it is recognised that the methods able to fully transform environmental assessment are still in the research phase and the practical tools which are needed for an integrated environmental, economic and social assessment of SUD are some years away. In the meantime, the web-based technology being developed by BEQUEST provides the communication and information systems required to undertake 'state-of-the-art' assessments. The decision support system being assembled provides the toolkit needed to undertake such assessments. This includes the assessment methods contained in the post-Brundtland directory and protocols to follow in using them as a means of qualifying whether the city of tomorrow has the capacity that is needed to carry its cultural heritage and evaluate if the forms of human settlement which surface from this process of urban development are sustainable.

Chapter 7

Valuation, Investment Appraisal, Discounting, Obsolescence and Depreciation: their Impact on the Urban Environment

Introduction

Focusing on the utility of property market valuation and investment appraisal, the following examines the critique of the discounting principle advanced by environmentalists. In particular, it examines the argument put forward regarding the link between the valuation and appraisal of investments, selection of a discount rate, existence of land use, building obsolescence and depreciation connected with the inter-generational downloading of costs. The link, seen by some, as having an adverse effect on the life cycle of land and buildings and as working against attempts to assess the impact experimental designs, aimed at energy saving, low carbon based emissions, have upon the environments in cities. Having examined the arguments, it goes on to rehabilitate the discounting mechanism by incorporating the market criteria of valuation and investment appraisal into the biophysics and ecology of life cycle analysis and environmental impact assessment.

The paper begins by examining the valuation and appraisal issue surrounding the discounting principle, reviews the life cycle and environmental impact assessment measures it is supposed to work against, even frustrate and exposes some of the contradictions in the position the critics set out. Having done this, it goes on to examine the sustainability requirement the (re)development of land uses and building programmes need to meet if they are to be environmentally-friendly and green in the manner they deal with obsolescence and depreciation. It shall then go on to show how the rejection of simple adjustments to the discount rate can be used to rehabilitate the mechanism into a co-evolutionary and multi-criteria approach to environmental economics. The paper will then go on to show how this rehabilitation of the discounting mechanism into such a form of environmental economics can produce a framework of analysis that has the potential to circumvent many of the criticisms about the utility of market based valuation and appraisal models.

By rejecting any 'simple adjustments' and producing a framework of analysis for a co-evolutionary and multi-criteria approach to valuation and investment appraisal, the paper illustrates how it is possible to circumvent the criticisms that the discounting mechanism has previously attracted and bridge the gap which has opened up between the property market and environmental economics of the, design and engineering of the construction sector. The paper shall propose this rehabilitation of the discounting principle into the mainstream of environmental economics is important, as criticisms of it by environmentalists have resulted in a gap opening up between the property markets underlying the (re)development of land uses, design, engineering and construction of building programmes incorporating the bio-physical and ecology components of energy conservation.

Time horizons, the spatial configuration and rate of redevelopment

In reference to the discounting principle, Harvey (1989: 97) points out that:

> In general terms (re)development takes place when the present value of the existing flow of future net returns from the existing use of land resources becomes less than the capital value of the cleared site.
>   We have therefore to calculate the present value of the land resources in their current use and compare this with the value of the cleared site, it must be emphasised that we are seeking to establish *capital net* return expected to be earned in future years, such returns must first be estimated and discounted for the present value and then aggregated.

From this initial statement on the discounting principle, Harvey (1989) formulates a simple income model of property valuation. In this model it is the notion of net annual returns, or what he refers to as NARs that take a leading role in the appraisal of investments and rate of (re)development in the time horizons and spatial configuration of land uses and building programmes (see also, Balchin, Bull and Kieve, 1995). As a form of income, the NAR is defined as the difference between gross annual returns (such as rent received) and operating costs (including repairs, maintenance, insurance and other such outgoings). To operationalise the notion of net income as an annual return in terms of property valuation and investment appraisal, he proposes that all gross annual returns and operating costs should be projected over the life-time of the land use, or building programme in question. Before subjecting the NARs to a rate of discount, he makes some comments on the nature of the relationship between the gross annual returns and operating costs. What he proposes is that over the life of the land use the gross annual return (GAR) will fall and operating costs will rise. He represents this notion as an annual return given by:

$$P = \sum_{t=i}^{n} \frac{R_i - O_i}{(1 + r)^i} \dots\dots\dots\dots\dots\dots\dots\dots\dots\dots\dots\dots\dots\dots\dots\dots\dots\dots\dots\dots\dots\dots\dots\dots\dots(1)$$

Where:

P   =   value of property in its current land use

n   =   period when GARs can be earned in its current use
Ri =   GARs from i to year n
Oi =   operating costs, excluding obsolescence and depreciation, from i to year n
r   =   rate of discount

It is a formula which represents the valuation of property as a method of investment appraisal and procedure that should be followed in the discounting of returns and calculation of present value. In terms of cleared site value, it is proposed that the value of the cleared site is equal to the present value of the most profitable alternative use, less the cost of clearing the site and rebuilding for the new use. The residual method of property valuation and procedure to be followed in the appraisal of investments required for this calculation is represented in the formula:

$$C = \sum_{t=i}^{n} \frac{R'_i - O'_i}{(1+r)^i} - D - B \dots\dots\dots\dots\dots\dots\dots\dots\dots\dots\dots\dots\dots\dots\dots \quad (2)$$

Where:

C   =   the value of the cleared site
n   =   period when GARs can be earned until alternative use
Ri =   GARs from i to year n
Oi =   operating costs, excluding obsolescence and depreciation, from i to year n
r   =   rate of discount
D   =   the cost of demolition and clearing the site
B   =   the cost of rebuilding to the new, alternative land use

The dynamics of the NAR model

Taking the NAR model to represent the dynamics of (re)development, it is possible to illustrate the process of change within the time-horizon of land-uses and spatial configuration of building programmes (see Figure 7.1). As Figure 7.1 illustrates, from year R the value of the cleared site is positive and increasing and eventually at T it is seen to exceed the present value of the land in its current use. As a result redevelopment takes place in year T, where PV equals VCS.

As Harvey (1989) is keen to point out, at T the land use is still technically efficient, for it can receive a NAR until year Z. However, in year T it becomes inefficient in economic terms because resources can be redeployed, or switched to an alternative, new land use having a higher present value. As he points out, under these circumstances the present value of the current and cleared site bring about a situation where the time-horizon of a land use is represented as OT and position whereby it is possible to calculate how many years the technical and economic life of a building programme is efficient.

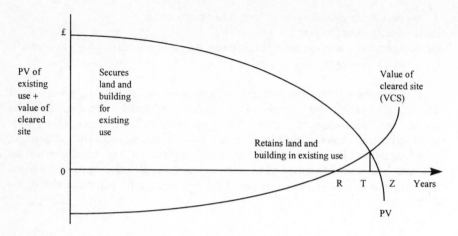

Figure 7.1   The Timing of Re-development

Under normal circumstances the spatial configuration of land uses are found to be concentrated in the city centre and that any alternative, new use which follows from a programme of building takes the form of an expansion from the centre to the periphery (Harvey, 1989, 1996).

With regards to the rate of redevelopment, it is stressed this is far more difficult to predict and is contingent on a number of factors. First the level of demand from occupiers and investors; second: operating costs and thirdly: the rate of interest. Ignoring the first two categories, he goes on to examine the effect a change in the rate of interest has on the present value of current land uses, cleared sites, time-horizon and spatial configuration of building programmes.

Land use, building obsolescence and depreciation

Perhaps the most obvious and immediate significance of this examination is that it introduces a variable not yet taken into account in the NAR model of property valuation and investment appraisal i.e. obsolescence and depreciation. However it should be recognised that the significance of obsolescence is much deeper than the addition of further expenditures on the cost of outgoings associated with land use and building programmes. This is because it represents the outcome of a much deeper enquiry into the adoption of discount rates, the so-called initial yield and nature of uncertainty and risk in property valuation and investment appraisal. As an approach to the valuation of property and appraisal of investment, the income thesis draws upon Fisher's (1965) representation of the discounting principle and interest payments the investment of capital yields in terms of a 'rate of return'. Such payments are seen to represent a return for: (a) the loss of liquidity; the payment for the foregoing of immediate consumption and switching of capital into investment. A payment also referred to as the 'risk free rate' because it represents the payment for the forgoing of consumption -- investment of capital in riskless operations unaffected by inflation; (c) anticipated inflation and compensation for the loss of real value; (d) the premium which reflects the degree of risk associated with a particular investment opportunity.

Based on this Fisher's (1965) theory of interest, the rate of return is represented as:

$$R = 1 + i + p$$

Where:

1 = Loss of liquidity
i = anticipated inflation
p = the risk premium.

Given the valuation of property and appraisal of investment does not allow for real rates of return, only notional, it is proposed there is no requirement for i and R can be represented as the sum of $1 + p$. Responding to Gordon (1982) and adding in rental growth to the equation, a risk, growth and deprecation explicit model of property valuation as a rational pricing mechanism in the appraisal of investments is put forward (see Baum and Crosby, 1988, 1995). This is represented as follows:

$$K = RFR + r^* - g + d$$

Where:

K = the initial yield on capital investment
RFR = the risk free, inflation prone opportunity cost rate of return
r^* = risk premium
g = expected annual rate of rental growth in new land uses and building programmes
d = depreciation in the capital component of land use i.e. the building and not the land. This is because land is seen to represent the non-reproducible resource that commands a scarcity value and transfer earnings payment from (re)development potential. This can, of course, be severely restricted if the land in question is subject to contamination and becomes obsolete in the sense it represents an environmental hazard.

Here the risk-free, inflation prone opportunity cost rate of return is taken to be the redemption yield on government securities and the premium is the additional return for investment of capital in property. The proposal for g to represent the expected annual rate of rental growth in new land uses and building programmes is made so as to allow the depreciation component to be measured in terms of the obsolescence a particular use, or programme has been subject to.

The formula is important for two reasons. First, K is equivalent to the r in the NAR model previously referred to. Looked at in this way, r appears to be a far more complex figure than initially thought. It appears, however, to be one it is necessary to live with if the criticisms of the model's silence on such matters as uncertainty, risk, rental growth and depreciation are to be overcome. Secondly, in taking the form of a summation equation (one which takes the first three criticisms into account), it also works within the definitions of physical deterioration, technical, economic and environmental obsolescence, put forward by the RICS, ISVA and Centre for Advanced Land Use Studies (CALUS) to explain the causes of depreciation. Causal factors Baum (1991, 94) is of the opinion are impossible to single out, but can be represented in terms of (a) physical deterioration (b) external appearance (c) internal specification and (d) configuration. Factors which Baum (1991, 94) argues need to be weighted in order of significance so that the impact of low and high flexibility can be analysed in terms of the impact depreciation has on rental values, yields, expenditure and risk.

The debate over life cycle analysis and environmental impact assessment

The previous discussion sought to identify that a number of developments have taken place in property valuation and investment appraisal which circumvent many of the criticisms aimed at the NAR model. In particular the fact that by substituting the r of NAR model in the valuation of property with that of the initial yield (shown by symbol K) in the obsolescence and depreciation sensitive model of investment appraisal, it is possible to be not only risk and growth explicit, but (obsolescence and) depreciation explicit too. Balanced against this, however, is the fact that this reformulation of r in terms of the initial yield has little to say about the time-horizons, spatial configuration of land uses, or building programmes. What is also noticeable is the tendency for both approaches to say little, if anything about whether or not they represent a net benefit or make a contribution to welfare. This question is, of course, looked at briefly under the issue surrounding rate of return over cost. But given neither of the approaches address spill-over effects, or externalities in any way whatsoever, it has to be recognised any claims in this department have to be balanced against the fact the discount rate (in whatever forms of surfaces i.e. the r of the NAR models, the K of the initial yield, or the plain old rate of interest!) are private and in that sense reflect private as opposed to social time preferences regarding the marginal productivity of capital. This is worth reiterating because it is the life cycle analysis issue of time-horizons, spatial configurations, spillovers, externalities and the social dimension of the discounting principle (and the way it ought to influence valuation and investment appraisal) that is of particular concern to those with an interest in environmental impact assessment (for example; Rydin, 1992; Vale, 1993; Brehney, 1993 respectively).

Working within these terms of reference, Rydin (1992:230) has sought to examine the life cycle and environmental impact assessment issues of valuation and investment appraisal in market economies. Quoting Pearce and Turner (1990), it is proposed that:

> the use of discounting downgrades costs to future generations at the expense of benefits to the current generation. Thus the expense of future maintenance will have a relatively smaller impact on the value of an investment compared with current capital expenditure. This form of valuation can inhibit many forms of refurbishment which would enhance energy conservation and undervalue buildings which minimise their environmental impact.

The contradiction, Rydin (1992) seeks to expose is that the economics of discounting in valuation and investment appraisal, tends to work against the possibility of introducing experimental designs aimed at low carbon and fossil fuel content because the benefits they provide in long term, repair, maintenance and running costs do not translate into any additional rental income, or a favourable yield adjustment, but merely additional capital costs. This is seen as contradictory because: (a) the so-called tyranny of the discounting principle tends to militate against the introduction of such experimental designs; (b) it inhibits improvements and refurbishments aimed at low carbon, fossil fuels consumption; (c) it leads to high repair, maintenance and overall running costs without any compensatory income; (d) tends to negate the possibility of offsetting deterioration, obsolescence and depreciation in a manner that brings about long term horizons and more compact spatial configurations; (e) downloads private and social costs associated with land use and building programmes to future generations for the benefit of the current. As a critique of the discounting principle, it draws upon the research of Pearce and Turner (1990). As it is a concern that leads Rydin (1992) to advocate a lower discount rate, initial yield or level of interest for environmentally-friendly, green land use and building programmes, it is a critique which requires further attention.

Pearce and Turner's (1990) criticism of the discounting principle is five-fold: (a) that private individuals can measure the pure time preference for present consumption as opposed to future investments; (b) the lack of consideration given by the marginal efficiency theory of capital to social time preference; (c) the lack of any specific allowance for uncertainty and risk in the choice of the discount rate; (d) the tendency to ignore that a positive, initial yield or rate of interest on capital investment assumes growth; (e) the fact that discount rates have an in built tendency to place a high value on current income and a low weighting to future capital and revenue costs.

Looked at independently, it is evident that the first four criticisms are economic in nature. What is also clear is that the last point has little to do with efficiency and in referring to such matters as the downloading of inter-generational costs, is a social question to do with equity. Irrespective of this however, what Pearce and Turner (1990: 223) recognise is that:

> The implication of the criticisms is that we should lower discount rates from whatever they are… . If we accept this we have an immediate problem in that the criticisms do not

tell us by how much we should lower discount rates. We are left with an indeterminate theory of discount rate selection.

In an attempt to circumvent this problem, Pearce and Turner (1990) propose that an alternative to the question of adjusting discount rates should be looked at. It is proposed that attention should focus not so much on the adjustment to the discount rate, but on the sustainability requirement valuation and investment appraisal needs to meet in order for it to take account of the effect land use, building obsolescence and depreciation have on the environment of cities. The 'appraisal' , that is to say, which is needed to account for such a situation and lead to a position where life cycle analysis and environmental impact assessment have the time-horizon and spatial configuration needed. The time-horizon and spatial configuration needed for the introduction of experimental designs, aimed at low carbon and fossil fuel content, because the benefits they provide in long term operating costs, repair and maintenance, obsolescence and depreciation, translates into additional rental income and a more sustainable yield.

The contradictions

The paper suggests that there exist a number of contradictions in the environmentalist's critique of the discounting principle which lies behind the valuation and appraisal of investments. The contradictions in question take a number of forms. First factual inaccuracies regarding the discounting principle in property valuation and investment appraisal. Secondly, the tendency to abandon NAR type models of valuation, investment appraisal and their use of efficiency as a measurement of environmental improvement, without any suitable replacement. Thirdly, the tendency to bracket questions of efficiency and environmental improvements within a given distribution of income, in favour of matters concerning the social equity of inter-generational downloading.

Rydin's (1992) criticism of the discounting principle in the valuation of property and appraisal of investments represents it as being at odds with, or working against the possibility of having time-horizons and spatial configurations of land-use and building programmes (as part of a (re)development process) whose effect on the environment of cities is ever going to be as capable of meeting the sustainability requirement. To support this line of reason, Rydin (1992) draws upon the critique of the discounting principle advanced by Pearce and Turner (1990): in particular the criticisms regarding the lack of due consideration given to the marginal efficiency of capital, social time preference, uncertainty, risk and question of growth. What, however, is most noticeable is that Pearce and Turner (1990) do not agree with the arguments put forward to support a discount rate adjustment, but instead focus attention on what they refer to as the sustainability requirement of valuation and investment appraisal. Based on this there can be no simple assumption (as Rydin, 1992 appears to make) that the possible benefits of life cycle analysis and impact assessment for environmentally-friendly, green land uses and building programmes, call for downward adjustments to discount rates, increase in capital value to offset additional expenditure on longer time-horizons and more compact spatial configurations: something which somehow and in some way, is seen to bring about a situation where the marginal productivity of capital in terms of income return over cost, yields a rate of interest that equates private individual with social time preference for environmentally-friendly, green technologies. However, even putting this to one side, it is evident that Pearce and Turner' s (1990) criticisms do not take into account the significant advances which have been made with regards to valuation and investment appraisal in the contemporary era. For you only have to look at the Fisher inspired formula for the initial yield of Baum (1991) and Baum and MacGregor (1992) to see that in the contemporary era valuation and investment appraisal does take uncertainty and risk into consideration and also acknowledges that growth is another component in the rate of interest (also, see Baum and Crosby, 1988, 1995). Indeed if we follow this line of reason through, it soon becomes clear that any downward adjustment to the rate of discount is based on the assumption the valuation and appraisal of investments will give rise to land uses and building programmes which are not only more efficient, or bring about an environmental improvement, but a level of growth sufficient enough (relative to obsolescence and depreciation) to sustain the yield as a rate of interest on the capital in question. It in fact *assumes a lower level of risk and high rate of growth*, a situation that *tends to draw additional, not fewer, scarce, fixed and finite resources into the (re)development process*. It is perhaps for this reason that Pearce and Turner (1990) draw the conclusion that the criticism of the discounting principle indicates there is something 'a miss' with the rates of return selected, but 'does not add up to much' and choose instead to focus attention on meeting the sustainability requirement.

Meeting the sustainability requirement

As O'Brian, Doig and Clift's (1996) contribution to the debate points out, the 'meeting of the sustainability requirement', is what most of the discussions on the critical role of valuation and investment appraisal have in common. As they also suggest, where these debates differ is in the method each proposes should be adopted for such purposes. As O'Brian, Doig and Clift (1996) also go on to point out, the main reason for rejecting the methodology of valuation and investment appraisal rests in the belief they suffer from the tyranny of the discounting principle, are in that sense too abstract, over-generalised and unhelpful in the way they represent the technical analysis which are needed to measure the effect (re)developments have upon the environment of cities. This understanding is - if a little less explicitly - also reflected in the rejection of market models as the basis of life cycle analysis and environmental impact assessment. The difficulty with this rejection of market-based models is that it is founded upon a incomplete, somewhat questionable critique of the discounting principle and which on reflection adds up to little more than a suggestion the abstract and over-generalised nature of valuation and investment appraisal means it is not possible for a detailed life cycle analysis or environmental impact assessment to meet the sustainability requirement. If it can be accepted that there are a number of contradictions in the critique of the discounting principle which leave the question of a meaningful relationship between valuation, investment appraisal and the environment open, then it becomes worthwhile searching for a means to bridge the gap that exists between the market basis of the former and more bio-physical cum ecological representations of the latter (Deakin, 1996, 1997c).

The rejection of simple adjustments

The rejection of any simple adjustments to the discount rate and plea to establish whether a development meets the sustainability requirement is also echoed in the work of Norgaard (1984), Perrings (1991), Norgaard and Howarth (1991). Here any notion of simple adjustments to discount rates is discouraged. This is because in principle such a course of action is seen as too mechanistic, unable in that sense to represent either the uncertainty, risk, growth, or knock-on obsolescence and depreciation, resulting from decisions of this kind (see Norgaard and Howarth, 1991 in particular).

Pearce and Turner (1991) and Pearce and Warford (1993), tend to see such concern over the choice of discount rate as too reminiscent of the debates over the valuation and appraisal dimension of cost benefit analysis (see Pearce, 1971, 1972). For Pearce (1990) an investigation of discounting in the context of valuation and appraisal appears to be of little interest (also see, Pearce and Markadya, 1989). Pearce instead turns attention to the valuation and appraisal of what is referred to as natural capital. Built upon a green accounting mechanism, natural capital is put forward as a instrument that captures the fixed, finite nature of those resources critical to the environmental integrity of ecosystems and whose depletion needs to be regulated so that the income stream resulting from the economic development of such resources grows at a rate which is sustainable. Grows, that is, at a rate whereby any factor substitution of natural for man-made capital, or replacement of such resources, does not result in a situation where the development in question brings about an inter-generational downloading of costs (Duborg and Pearce, 1996).

Given the complex nature of the relationship between the environment and economy, uncertainty and incalculable nature of the risk related to decisions about environmental conservation and economic growth, considerations about the choice of discount rate tend to be seen as of little help in the valuation and appraisal of investment. Instead attention turns to the use of non-standard (hedonic and contingency type) valuations (Powell, Pearce and Craighill, 1997) deployment of life cycle analysis and environmental impact assessment in the appraisal process and the effect such instruments can have upon the index of sustainable development (Facheaux, Pearce and Proops, 1996).

In providing a critique of natural capital as a green accounting mechanism, Facheaux and O'Conner (1998), suggest Pearce's 'environmentally-friendly, green' response to the problem of valuation and investment appraisal *merely reframes the question and does not provide a solution* (see, also O'Conner, 1998).

Facheaux and O'Conner (1998) stress the need for what they term non-monetary valuations. Instead of searching for a monetary valuation of natural capital and appraisal of the effect any such development has upon the index of sustainability, Facheaux and O'Conner (1998) put the environment before the economy in what they term a co-evolutionary approach. What they suggest is that the development of both environmental and economic goods/services are complementary, not in the way environmental conservation can sustain economic growth, but quality of life per se. This focus on the quality of life shifts attention to the environment in terms of ecosystem integrity, carrying capacity, degradation, waste, pollution etc. and the scientific basis of any such valuation and appraisal. Here attention turns to energy and the laws of thermo-dynamics in understanding the environment in such non-monetary terms. For Facheaux and O'Conner (1998), energy represents the standard measure of value, as this is the only universal component common to all development, irrespective of environmental context, economic system, appraisal, techniques of analysis, assessment methods etc.

It is the physics of energy that is of particular interest for Facheaux and O'Conner (1998), who seek to apply it in the bio-physical context of ecosystems and given the connection they use for such purposes is both life cycle analysis and environmental impact assessment, it is evident they seek to unite the bio-physical with the social sciences through a particular emphasis on the non-monetary (ecological-based), as opposed to monetary (i.e. market, hedonic and contingency) tradition in the valuation and appraisal of such developments. In casting attention back on energy, eco-systems, life cycle analysis and environmental impact assessment, the point of emphasis shifts away from the economic development of income streams and conservation of resources, to the inter-generational downloading of costs. The reason for this lies in Facheaux and O'Conner (1998) belief that the two discourses (i.e. bio-physical and social) in environmental economics can be reconciled through a multi-criteria analysis which applies the so-called 'hard' certainties of bio-physical science to the more uncertain, risky social relations, 'softer' and by nature more difficult to predict. Rather than represent the moneterisation of income streams in the face of uncertainty and risk as incalculable, due to the inter-generational down loading of costs associated with the hazards of growth, obsolescense and depreciation, what they do is apply the certainties of the non-monetary (bio-physical and ecological-based issues) to assess the impact any (re)development of land uses and building programmes (and economic growth in general) has upon the environment.

What Facheaux and O'Conner (1998) do is rehabilitate concerns over: money, energy, income, costs, uncertainty, risk, growth, obsolescence, depreciation, time and space, into a form of environmental economics that allows (re)development to be assessed in terms of the impact any inter-generational downloading has on the index of sustainable development. This is done by placing emphasis upon the biophysical and social in the co-evolutionary approach to hard and soft issues in the environmental economics of a multi-criteria (monetary and non-monetary) valuation and appraisal of life cycles and impact assessments (see also, Voogd, 1983; Massam, 1988; Nijkamp, Rietveld and Voogd, 1990; Grillenzoni,

Ragazzoni, Bazzani and Canavari, 1997). The significance of this rehabilitation is as follows:

- valuation and investment appraisal is still a major issue in terms of understanding the effects land-use development and building programmes have upon the environment of cities;
- it proposes the valuation and appraisal in question ought to be co-evolutionary in nature, based upon a multi-criteria (monetary and non-monetary) analysis;
- such an analysis should rehabilitate concerns over money, energy, income, costs, uncertainty, risk, growth, obsolescence, depreciation, time and space;
- these concerns should form the basis of an economics that allows any such (re)development of land use and building programmes to be measured in terms of the effect they have on the environment of cities;
- such a from of environmental economics requires both life cycle analysis and environmental impact assessments;
- the concerns over money, energy, income, costs, uncertainty, risk, growth, obsolescence, depreciation, time and space, allow the *discounting mechanism of market valuation and non-standard hedonic and contingency forms of investment appraisal to co-exist and evolve along side the environmental economics of both life cycle analysis and environmental impact assessment*;
- this co-existence and evolution of the discounting mechanism (in the life cycle analysis and impact assessment of environmental economics) provides a means to establish whether the (re)development of land-uses and building programmes, with energy-saving, clean air technologies, is not only environmentally-friendly and green, but meets the sustainability requirement in the way it deals with the intergenerational downloading of costs.

Rehabilitating the discounting mechanism

While the aforementioned goes some way to rehabilitate the discounting mechanism into the valuation and appraisal of environmentally-friendly, green land uses and building programmes, the question about how to do this in the co-evolutionary logic of a multi-criteria approach still remains. The question that remains is whether the form of environmental economics in question should search for some universal standard of value i.e. the consumption of energy in the law of thermo-dynamics for the appraisal of development programmes? That is put the hard certainties of the biophysical and ecological-based issues first and the more uncertain, risky social relations which are 'softer' and by nature more difficult to predict, second. While the co-evolutionary logic of a multi-criteria analysis and assessment does not lay down any rules in this respect, it is possible to see the biophysical dimensions and ecology of energy (non-monetary themes) as *nesting* within the monetary (market, hedonic and contingency type valuation and investment appraisal). If we can accept the co-evolutionary and multi-criteria approach to valuation and investment appraisal allows this, then the virtues of an NAR-type model become apparent. The virtues in question are as follows:

- it has an implicit bio-physical and ecological dimension shown in the energy factor in the operation and maintenance costs, illustrated in Ri - Oi and represented as the enumerator in formulas (1) and (2). When supplemented with a life cycle analysis and impact assessment, the environmental economics of energy consumption become more explicit and can be represented not only in monetary terms, but its own universal standard of measure;
- a formal time and space dimension is built into the model and its formula for the selection of a discount rate which is risk, growth, obsolescence and depreciation explicit.

The main criticism that may be levelled at the model is the way the formula deals with risk and it in turn relates to obsolescence and depreciation. For what it does is represent risk in terms of systematic and specific market rather than environmental risk. However, as the search for environmental risk (in relation to growth, obsolescence and depreciation) is seen by both Debourg and Pearce (1997) and Facheaux and O'Conner (1998) as impractical without the assistance of life cycle analysis and impact assessments, this omission is perhaps not critical at this stage.

Towards a framework for analysis

So far it has been suggested that the debate over the application in the discounting principle in property valuation and investment appraisal has tended to become separated from issues concerning land use, building obsolescence, depreciation and effect the (re)development process has on the environment of cities. It has also been argued that any attempts to progress the matter should be grounded in the environmental economics of the discounting principle and draw upon what is understood about valuation methodology and investment techniques to advance our knowledge of obsolescence and depreciation via life cycle analysis and environmental impact assessment.

It is for this reason the paper proposes that a framework for analysis should be grounded in a form of environmental economics which provides the opportunity for a detailed examination of meaningful relationships between the dynamics of the time-horizons and spatial configurations of what have been referred to as land use, building obsolescence, depreciation and expenditure on experimental designs, aimed at the introduction of energy-saving, clean air technologies. That is, by undertaking an analysis of how obsolescence and depreciation reacts back on operating costs, repairs, maintenance, improvements etc. Or, from the NAR model's point of view, the relationships between (1 + r) and Oi. The relationship Rydin (1992) is critical of due to its apparent inability to produce land uses and building programmes with operating costs, repair schedules, maintenance programmes and refurbishments, aimed at low carbon, fossil fuel consumption. The relationship that also appears to be of particular interest to Vale (1993). Accepting that Rydin's (1992) criticisms and call for downward adjustments to r are not supported by Pearce and Turner (1990) and this leaves the whole question of the relationship between valuation, investment appraisal and the environment wide open, it is possible to argue the best way to further any common interest in the debate over the market basis, bio-physical and ecology of both life cycle analysis and environmental impact assessment (and in that sense the sustainability requirement), is through a closer examination of the relationship between Oi and r, the discount rate.

In terms of the NAR notion of net income, it is only possible at this stage to qualify the equation so that r represents K= RFR + r* - g + d. While this will be common for both equations (1) and (2), it will also affect Ri and Oi due to the fact r will be net of obsolescence and depreciation. While the modifications appear minor and perhaps insignificant, it is proposed that their true value lies in the fact the adjusted NAR model addresses many of the criticisms made about the tyranny of the discounting principle and selection of an appropriate rate, draws particular attention to both risk and growth in setting the return on capital *and makes it possible for the rate of interest to evolve from the life cycle analysis and environmental impact assessments undertaken rather than the other way around.* This is an important point, because tackled in this way it is not the market that sets its standards upon the environment, but the life cycle analysis and environmental impact assessment (i.e. environmental economics of the green contingent in the design, engineering and construction sector) whose valuation and appraisal produces the rate of interest acting as a return on capital. The following lists the potential benefits of any such examination:

(a) it would focus attention on the nature of the relationships between Oi and r in the NAR model;

(b) it would build upon the advances of contemporary property valuation and investment appraisals not only in terms of the income approach to risk and growth, but the cost based thesis (Deakin, 1997a, b) on outgoings associated with operating costs and capital expenditure on repairs, maintenance, improvements and refurbishments;

(c) the collection of information on such expenditure would augment our understanding of land-use, building obsolescence and depreciation, by using the criteria set out by Baum (1991, 1994) and Rydin (1992), to establish whether experimental designs of the type in question have notable benefits;

(d) it would also make it possible for the benefits of contemporary valuation and investment appraisal to be formally integrated into the field of development analysis - something it may be difficult to believe has not yet been delivered (Department of the Environment, 1991; Harou, Daly, Goodland, 1994; Deakin, 1996, 1997c; Brooks, Cheshire, Evans and Stabler, 1997);

(e) such data would also allow life cycle exercises to be undertaken in the valuation and appraisal of investments, obsolescence and depreciation and also be capable of incorporating an environmental impact assessment into the (re)development of land-uses and building programmes (Deakin, 1999a, b). This would also allow the market-based criteria of the adjusted NAR-type model to be integrated with the life cycle analysis and environmental impact assessments of BREEAM (see Cole, 1997; Cooper, 1997, 99; Cooper and Curwell, 1998). Here adjusted NAR-type models would provide the market criteria, whereas life cycle analysis and impact assessments like BREEAM, could provide the biophysics and ecology of energy conservation. Nesting within each other, the adjusted NAR-type model would be able to value in line with the market, while the standard for the conservation of energy could be represented in a universal form. The integration of the adjusted NAR-type model with that of life cycle analysis and environmental impact assessment would also add the valuation and investment currently absent from such an analysis or impact assessment (Birtles, 1997; Department of Environment, Transport and the Regions, 1999). This life cycle analysis and environmental impact assessment would provide the information to establish whether the (re)development proposal meets the sustainability requirement. His would be done by benchmarking the impact against a number of indicators to establish what effect the (re)development has on the downloading of costs and index of sustainability associated with such measurements (Mitchell, May and McDonald, 1995; May, Mitchell and Kupiszewska, 1997);

(f) such a schedule of costing would provide information for the valuation and appraisal of the initial capital and subsequent revenue expenditures in terms of outgoings associated with the energy-saving technologies of clean air. The effect of this on occupational demand for land uses and building programmes and demand for property due to its value as an investment opportunity could also be analysed;

(g) the with/without logic of comparative analysis could also be drawn upon to establish not so much the potential, but real effects of introducing such technologies. This would identify what value the market puts on such technologies. That is, what price, both users and investors are willing to pay for the income-benefits of a structure that does not download costs into the future. It would also demonstrate the cost of not taking such a course of action. Something which could be measured in terms of the different present values of those properties with and without the technologies in question. While, this does not account for the spillover, or external costs/benefits associated with such a course of action, it ought to be possible to satisfy this by some non-standard form of, hedonic, or contingency exercise (in this instance forming the basis of a life cycle analysis and environmental impact assessment) geared towards a willingness to accept the inter-generational loading in question. The effect this form of valuation, combining, as it does, both market and environmental criteria, has on the appraisal of investments would also need to be placed under examination;

(h) RFR + r* gives an indication of the parameters i.e. upper and lower levels of the discount rate, r, or initial yield K, whereas g provides an indication of anticipated growth. The significance of this being that both variables are linked into the capital markets of the economy and provide the opportunity to estimate the effect any change in the relationship between Oi and r will have not just upon the time-horizons and spatial configuration of land use and building programmes (for example; the income benefits of longer time-horizons, more compact spatial configurations, lower risk, greater growth and cost-savings) but in terms of the reduced rates of obsolescence and depreciation brought about by the introduction of experimental designs aimed at energy-saving, clean air technologies. In short a reduction in the costs of intergenerational downloading not only from a given land use or building programme, but city as a whole. The same is true for equation (2), but here the effect also extends into D and B;

(i) here again the effect of the cost of introducing such new technologies into the (re)development of land uses and building programmes could be analysed to establish at what point the income benefits become efficient in economic terms and socially equitable from the environmental point of view. Such an analysis would be in accordance with the policy towards longer term time-horizons and more compact spatial configurations for energy consumption in the use and land and buildings in the city (Breheny, 1992; Symes, 1997).

This list of considerations does not of course exhaust all the issues in question; it merely sets out a framework for analysis that makes it possible to circumvent many of the criticisms made about the discounting principle. The principle that underlies the NAR model of valuation and investment appraisal, its representation of the time-horizons and spatial configuration of land use, building obsolescence and depreciation. The time-horizons, spatial configuration, land use, building obsolescence and depreciation of particular concern to those with an interest in life cycle analysis and environmental impact assessment.

What this adjusted NAR-type model does is turn the principle of 'the polluter pays' around by introducing the means by which those agents of change in the market (i.e. designers, engineers, contractors, planners etc) can undertake the life cycle analysis and environmental impact assessments that *not only value, in market, bio-physical and ecological terms, the economic efficiency and social equity of such contributions to the marginal productivity of capital, but compensate them with a rate of return which is seen as fair and just from the environmental point of view. Without this and what is in effect an environmentally-friendly, green pricing mechanism*, it would not be possible to overcome the legacy of market failure in dealing with the environment and link the means with the ends i.e. the market basis of the valuation and investment appraisal underlying the adjusted NAR model, with the time-horizons and spatial configurations of environmentally-friendly, green technologies for land use and building programmes. That is, *show 'how it pays'*, in terms of the market and environment, to introduce energy-saving technologies with lower carbon-based emissions. Without this link it would not be possible to demonstrate the range of opportunities open for the state to finance experiments of this kind and show *the real value*, such land uses and building programmes offer the public for not only as a form of environmental conservation (be it in terms of energy, or natural capital consumption) capable of sustaining economic growth, but an enhanced quality of life.

Conclusions

This paper has examined the critique of the discounting principle environmentalists have made in relation to valuation investment appraisal and its application in the income based NAR model of land use time-horizons and the spatial configuration of building programmes. In particular it has looked at the link made between the selection of a discount rate, the valuation, appraisal of investment and the inter-generation downloading of costs associated with the use of land, repair, maintenance and refurbishment of buildings. In examining this debate it has found the criticism wanting. It has also sought to expose some of the contradictions within the arguments put forward. The argument that it is this downloading of cost which works against the introduction of experimental designs aimed at environmentally-friendly, green land uses and building programmes in particular. In doing so the paper has also sought to demonstrate the connection made between discounting, valuation, appraisal of investment and downloading of costs is tenuous and open to question.

In addition to this, it is hoped the paper provides a means to strengthen the relationship between life cycle analysis, environmental impact assessment, valuation and appraisal in the context of previous discussions surrounding such matters. With this in mind, it has sought to allay any fears those responsible for valuations and investment appraisals might have about using NAR type models. It has done this by focusing attention on the positive contribution market based valuations and investment appraisals can make to life cycle analysis and environmental impact assessment. This is an important point because given the undue criticism they have attracted there is some doubt about the utility of such models. The outcome of this being seen in the switch of attention away from NAR type models of market valuation and investment appraisal and towards the life cycle analysis and environmental impact assessments. Something, which in itself is questionable for the fact that it has left a gap between the market and environment.

Chapter 8

Evaluating the Development of Sustainable Communities

Introduction

The on-going review of structure plans in the United Kingdom has highlighted the attractiveness of new settlements as an alternative to cramming, peripheral expansion and urban sprawl. This chapter examines the argument for new settlements appearing in the Written Statement on Lothian's 1995 Structure Plan Review. It goes on to establish how the experiments going on in Edinburgh's South East Wedge are transforming the new settlement phenomenon in to the search for a plan-led, environmentally-friendly and sustainable pattern of settlement. It draws attention to the Interim Development Framework put in place to support the plan-led, environmentally-friendly experiment and settlement model adopted for such purposes. After making a number of observations on the development of sustainable communities in Edinburgh's South East Wedge, the paper draws some conclusions on the nature of the experiment.

The Written Statement

The 1995 Written Statement on the Lothian Structure Plan Review states: 'the development of Edinburgh can no longer be accommodated within the existing boundaries of the City'. The 'cramming of development in brown field sites is no longer an option for Edinburgh'. Neither is development by peripheral expansion around the edge of the City's greenbelt. There are 'simply not enough brown field sites to develop in Edinburgh and peripheral expansion around the edge of the City would put too much pressure on the greenbelt and result in urban sprawl' (p.14). The solution, the statement suggests, rests with the development of new settlements. In particular with the 'development of new settlements on a 1,600 hectare site at the periphery of Edinburgh and in an area of the City's greenbelt known as the South East Wedge' (p.15).

As an exercise in the management of growth, the statement suggests that plan-led experiments of this kind can protect the environment and the proposal to 'develop new settlements in the South East Wedge of Edinburgh provides the City with just such an opportunity' (p.15). The reasons put forward to explain why the development provides such an opportunity are as follow:

- representing less than 10% of the greenbelt, the site has the capacity to accommodate 35% of Edinburgh's land use requirements, 60% of the City's population growth, 15 per cent of additional households and 30% of future employment opportunities;
- the site has the capacity to carry such a level of growth due to spare capacity in both the utility and transportation networks and because it is already well serviced with out-of-town shopping centres, retail and warehouse parks, leisure and entertainment facilities;
- in releasing pressure for speculative development around the edge of the City and protecting the greenbelt, the site provides the opportunity for Edinburgh to make sure the use of land, utilities, transportation networks and both retail and leisure services, is environmentally-friendly and fosters a more sustainable pattern of settlement.

The case the Written Statement makes for the development of new settlements is compelling. It goes a long way to illustrate the strategic significance of the 1,600-hectare site in Edinburgh's South East Wedge. It suggests the South East Wedge offers Edinburgh an alternative to the speculative development of green field sites, the peripheral expansion that follows and urban sprawl which this produces. Why? Because it is seen to provide the opportunity for Edinburgh to plan the City's expansion into the greenbelt and protect the environment through the pattern of settlement it develops for such purposes.

The new settlement phenomenon

The development of such settlements is, of course, not as new a phenomenon as the title would suggest. As Ward (1992) establishes, with the privatisation of the New Towns Commission, private consortiums have sought to develop new settlements as an alternative to peripheral expansion and urban sprawl. It is a phenomenon that Glasson, Therivel and Chadwick (1994) also examine. Their research shows that during the review of structure plans carried out between 1988-1993, 46 new settlement proposals had been submitted to planning authorities throughout the UK and out of this only two developments were successful in receiving outline planning consent. As Ratcliff and Stubbs (1996) also note, while the tight fiscal regime local governments operated under during this period made the development of new settlements by private consortiums attractive, they were too speculative, not supported by the planning system and unable to allay any fears the public had about their impact on the environment.

It is noticeable that the proposal to develop new settlements in Edinburgh's South East Wedge goes a long way to avoid the difficulties experienced by many of its predecessors. Not only is it supported by a written statement, but also it proposes to be plan-led and environmentally-friendly. While going a long way to distinguish the development of new settlements in Edinburgh from previous experiments of this type, it is not these qualities that· mark it out from its predecessors. As a more advanced experiment in the modelling of alternatives to peripheral expansion and urban sprawl, the qualities that distinguish the proposal to develop new settlements in the South East Wedge from its predecessors are to be found elsewhere. It is the proposal to develop a pattern of settlement that is sustainable which distinguishes the experiment going on in Edinburgh from its predecessors. This is because in the South East Wedge the object of the exercise is not the development of new settlements per se, but that of an environmentally-friendly pattern of settlement which is sustainable.

Towards sustainable settlement patterns

The shift of emphasis from new settlements and towards the development of environmentally-friendly settlement patterns which are sustainable does have a purpose. It is done to highlight how the experiments going on in Edinburgh are transforming the new settlement phenomenon. What it illustrates is that the new settlement phenomenon is no longer about the speculative development of green field sites. It shows that in the South East Wedge, the new settlement phenomenon has been transformed into an experiment about the management of growth in the green belt which is plan-led, environmentally-friendly and produces a sustainable pattern of settlement. This transformation of the new settlement phenomenon is important for another reason. It is important because it identifies the plan-led, environmentally-friendly pattern of settlement that Edinburgh proposes to develop in the South East Wedge, advances a settlement pattern which is sustainable in the sense it provides an alternative to peripheral expansion and urban sprawl.

The Interim Development Framework

The search for a pattern of settlement that is sustainable is a matter which the 1996 Interim Development Framework (IDF) addresses (Chesterton, 1996). Here attention turns to the question of how to design such a settlement pattern. How, that is, to design a pattern of settlement which has a distinctive urban culture, spatially compact form and is able to develop as a set of sustainable communities? The question that follows on is: and how in turn to use the said development as a means of modelling an environmentally-friendly settlement pattern which represents an alternative to peripheral expansion around the edge of the City and urban sprawl this produces? The settlement model which the document puts forward as the framework for the development of the South East Wedge addresses these two questions.

The claim, that the settlement model which the document puts forward is plan-led and environmentally-friendly, is based upon how the IDF makes use of and draws upon the Department of the Environment's (DoE's) Planning Research Programme. In particular the studies of:

- growth and the green belt (DoE, 1993a)

- alternative settlement patterns (Breheny, Gent and Lock, 1993)
- infrastructure service provision (transport in particular) report prepared by the DoE (1993b)

In England and Wales the said research programme provides the basis for the Planning Guidance Notes (PGN's) and in Scotland these notes appear in the form of the National Planning Policy Guidelines (NPPG's). In Scotland the research provides the basis for the following:

- NPPG 1 (The Planning System) and its policy guidance on growth management, green belts, environmental protection and the development of sustainable settlement patterns;
- use of the aforesaid to ensure that such a form of plan-led development is environmentally-friendly in the sense which it is consistent with *This Common Inheritance* (HM Government, 1990, 1991, 1994a);
- incorporation of statements made about environmental planning in *Sustainable Development: The UK Strategy* (HM Government, 1994b) into such plan-led developments;
- adoption of the aforementioned into the on-going review of structure plans;
- use of strategic environmental assessment to ensure policies on growth management and the use of green belts to protect the environment, are consistent with the aforementioned documents (DoE, 1991, 1993c) and;
- use of the DoE's (1993c) *Environmental Appraisal of Development Plans,* to carry out such assessments and provide statements on growth management, use of the green belt and protection of the environment.

Drawing upon this plan-led and environmentally-friendly framework for the development of sustainable communities in Edinburgh's South East Wedge, the IDF document goes on to outline the settlement model which it proposes should be adopted for such purposes.

The settlement model

The settlement model the document puts forward as a design solution appears under the heading of 'sustainable communities'. Under this heading attention is drawn to the principles of sustainable development which the document argues such settlements should be based upon. Modelling the development of sustainable communities, the document proposes that Edinburgh's experiment in managing growth through plan-led, environmentally-friendly settlement patterns in the South East Wedge, should be based on the following:

- a distinctive urban culture;
- a spatially compact form;
- a strong landscape framework in a countryside setting;

- a set of neighbourhoods;
- a high density of population;
- a balance of land use, economic and social structures;
- an energy conscious public transportation network;
- high levels of infrastructure and shared service provision;
- a pattern of settlement that is able to integrate existing communities with those emerging from the development and ;
- a financial structure that is viable in the short, medium and long term horizon.

These qualities reflect the findings of Breheny (1992a, 1992b), Breheny and Rookwood (1993) and Breheny, Gent and Lock's (1993) studies of alternative settlement patterns.

Developing sustainable communities

The proposal to develop a distinctive urban culture is defined in terms of what it represents as an alternative settlement model. That is as an urban culture which represents an alternative to the suburban lifestyle. The suburban lifestyle whose particular brand of resource intensive consumerism expands into the periphery and demands the speculative development of green field sites around the edge of the city. The speculative development of sites that in turn requires local authorities to release land from the greenbelt and which experience suggests, leads to the coalescence of settlements around the edge of the city. The coalescence of settlements that in turn results in a loss of identity and which leads to the break up of communities under the process of urban sprawl.

In proposing to counter the coalescence, loss of identity and break up of communities associated with such forms of peripheral expansion, the model suggests that the City needs to manage growth in a way which is plan-led, environmentally-friendly and which produces a distinctive urban culture for the spatially compact forms of settlement it proposes to develop. Drawing on the experiences of alternative settlements throughout the UK, the IDF document suggests that if alternatives to peripheral expansion and urban sprawl are to produce settlement patterns which develop as sustainable communities, they should have: distinctive urban characters, spatially compact forms, strong landscape frameworks in county side settings, relatively high population densities, mixed land uses, balanced economic and social structures and provide energy conscious public transportation systems (see Owens, 1992; Breheny, 1995; Selman 1996; Brown, 1998). The other qualities listed (high levels of infrastructure, shared service provision, pattern of settlement that is able to integrate existing communities with those emerging from the development and have a financial structure which is viable in the short, medium and long term horizon), are studied by Hall and Ward (1998). In this study attention is drawn to the development of such settlements in the Thames Corridor, cities of Cambridge and Peterborough. Here particular attention is drawn to the integrative qualities of such settlements and tight fiscal regime under which they operate. In particular the fact that the fiscal regime which operates for the development of such settlements requires a number of disclosures to be made about their financial viability (Hall and Ward, 1998).

Sustainable communities in Edinburgh's South East Wedge

In Edinburgh this alternative to suburban culture is seen to surface from the decision to restrict development around the edge of the City and to concentrate it on a 1,600 hectare green field site known as the South East Wedge. This particular process of peripheral expansion is seen to be plan, rather than market-led and environmentally-friendly in the sense that the settlement pattern will have a distinctive urban culture, take on a spatially compact form and discount the possibility which exists for the development to result in any coalescence, loss of identity and break up of communities in this part of the City's greenbelt.

The strong landscape framework and countryside setting which the model proposes is seen to provide the means by which to guard against the possibility of any such coalescence. This is because the model proposes that the development should make use of natural features, woodlands and country parks as a way of keeping settlements separate from one another. Such features are proposed to separate the peripheral housing estate and former mining village forming the existing settlements, from the neighbourhoods which the model also proposes should form the focus of the development

The possibility of this peripheral expansion resulting in infill development, coalescence of settlements and loss of identity is discounted through the measures which the model puts forward for the communities in question. This is because the settlement model proposes to subject the peripheral housing estate to an urban regeneration programme and advocates a limited town centre expansion scheme for the former mining village. The proposal to keep the existing settlements physically separated from the new development also surfaces as a major theme when considering the rest of the site. Here it is proposed that up to 20,000 people should be accommodated within three new settlements. While 'clustered' around each other, the model suggests the 5,000 additional households forming the development should be physically separated from one another as neighbourhoods. Having a high population density (forecast to be between 50 and 200 per hectare), it is proposed that these neighbourhoods should have a balanced set of land uses. The balanced mix of land uses proposed comprises land for residential, commercial (light industrial, business, warehouse and distribution and retail) use and communal services (transportation, recreational, education and health). The design also allows for the neighbourhood units to have a balanced (low, middle and upper income) economic and social structure.

Living and working environment

In the interests of providing a 'high quality working and living environment', the model allows for the development to have an energy conscious transportation system. It suggests the transportation system should incorporate a number of measures: for example; a public transport corridor, bus priority proposal, park and ride system and traffic calming scheme. It also suggests that some of the neighbourhoods should be car free and that residents ought to be within easy walking distance of public transport facilities.

Infrastructure requirements

The infrastructure requirements are considerable. They include land consolidation works, sites and service provision, transportation, recreation, education and health provision. In view of this, the model proposes the transportation, recreation, education and health services should be shared between the peripheral housing estate, former mining village and neighbourhoods forming the settlement pattern it puts forward for the development of sustainable communities. This is because the neighbourhoods emerging from the development will not be able to provide either the employment, recreational, education, health or retail services needed to support the high quality working and living environment the model suggests is needed for the development of sustainable communities. It is this sharing of the infrastructure and service provision that is seen to represent the key factor integrating the peripheral housing estate, former mining village and neighbourhoods into a settlement pattern which is sustainable. Into a pattern of settlement that is sustainable in the sense which the regenerated peripheral housing estate, expanded former mining village and neighbourhoods have access to, share and co-operate in providing the infrastructures and services needed for the high quality living and working environments forming the settlement pattern to discount any possibility of coalescence, loss of identity and break up of communities resulting from this process of peripheral expansion.

Financial viability

The financial viability issue tackles particular difficulties associated with the geology of the site and high level of both infrastructure and service provision needed for the settlement pattern to develop. Given the abnormal preparation costs, high infrastructure and service content, the framework sets out what the development will yield in the form of land receipts. The cash flows making up these land receipts are analysed over the short, medium and long-term horizons and discounted at the opportunity cost of capital. The income takes the form of receipts from the sale of sites making up the mixed set of land uses (residential, light industrial and retail). The income represents the development value of the sites with planning permission. The costs include the purchase of land at existing use value (i.e. without the development proposal) and capital expenditure on the infrastructures required to service the sites. The existing use value is taken to represent the sum of agricultural and 'hope value'. The capital expenditure represents the cost of site preparation, providing the recreation, education, health and public transportation network. The discounted cash flow analysis supporting the appraisal illustrates the project should yield an 11 per cent internal rate of return (i.e. surplus of income over cost of development).

As a development appraisal, the exercise follows the guidelines set out in the DOE's (1991) publication on *Policy Appraisal and the Environment.* It also makes use of DOE's (1993) document on *Making Markets Work for the Environment* and publication from the Local Government Management Board (LGMB, 1994) on *Greening Economic Development.* Drawing upon these sources a number of economic instruments: for example, cash flow analysis, discounting procedures and cost benefit analysis techniques, are made us of to establish whether the quality of the working and living environments making up the development, produce enough planning gain for the land market to fund the infrastructure services upon which the settlement pattern is based and the sustainable communities are seen to rest.

Some observations

From the aforesaid, it is evident the growth management strategy adopted for Edinburgh's South East Wedge is clearly plan-led. It proposes the development of green field sites need not be speculative, can be plan-led and this in turn provides the opportunity for such experiments to be environmentally-friendly. This is because the distinct urban culture of the spatially compact forms it puts forward as a design solution, provides a settlement pattern which protects the green belt, guards against coalescence, loss of identity and any possible break up of communities resulting from the subsequent pressure for infill development.

Having said this, it should perhaps also be noted that the degree to which this form of plan-led experiment can be said to be environmentally-friendly is difficult to establish. Whether the plan-led experiment is environmentally-friendly, or merely an attempt to 'green economic development' is perhaps the question in hand. This is because some observers of the new settlement phenomenon suggest such plan-led experiments are environmentally-friendly and others see them as little more than an attempt to 'gloss over' such issues and green economic development (see, Selman, 1996 and Davoudi, 1997, respectively for a representation of such positions). As Gibbs et al (1996) point out, whatever position is taken on the issue it is a matter that raises questions about the integration of the environmental and economic in the development of sustainable communities. Given the experiment currently going on in the South East Wedge of Edinburgh proposes to provide a model for managing growth that is not only plan-led and environmentally-friendly, but offers a design solution which is also efficient in greening economic development, the question of integration is one of particular significance.

The environmentally-friendly nature

The immediate difficulties we face in trying to establish the development's environmentally-friendly nature, rests with the effective absence of the data needed for such an assessment. This is because:

- despite drawing upon the DOE's Planning Research Programme and using NPPG 1 to guide the on-going review of the structure plan, strategic environmental assessments and appraisals of how to manage growth, the IDF document provides very little evidence to support the claim that the plan-led development produces an environmentally-friendly settlement pattern;
- while placing a great deal of emphasis on the capacity the site has to carry a distinctive urban culture in spatially compact forms, set within strong landscape frameworks and countryside settings, the model and design solution it puts forward offers no formal assessment of its ecological footprint, bio-diversity, or natural capital.

In its current form the model and design solution it puts forward, is vulnerable to many of the criticisms Glasson, Therivel and Chadwick (1994) and Ratcliff and Stubbs (1996), have previously made about the new settlement phenomena and the sometimes less than friendly way which plan-led developments of this kind treat the environment. These criticisms are also echoed by Lichfield (1996). The criticisms suggest that little has been learnt about the environmental values of the urban culture, spatially compact forms, strong landscape framework and countryside setting which the model sets out, or how this in turn leads to a position where the design of the neighbourhoods, population densities, socio-economic structures, energy conscious public transport, high levels of both infrastructure and service provision, produce an efficient greening of economic development. An efficient greening of economic development that is financially viable and which is in turn taken to represent an environmentally-friendly pattern of settlement for the development of sustainable communities (also see, Beatley, 1995; Campbell, 1996; Cosgriff and Steinmann, 1998).

Little more than an aesthetic?

Set against the critique of such models and the design solutions they advance, the environmentally-nature of the settlement pattern might be seen to add up to little more than an aesthetic. An aesthetic that reduces the environmental value of ecologically sound designs to the distinctive urban culture, spatially compact forms, strong landscape framework and countryside setting which the model sets out. An aesthetic about the design of neighbourhoods, population densities, land uses, socio-economic structures and public transportation systems which form the infrastructures required to service high quality living and working environments. The high quality living and working environments that are friendly because the land market upon which they rest produces enough planning gain to efficiently green the economic development of the peripheral housing estate, former mining village and neighbourhoods. Efficiently green the economic development of the said estate, village and neighbourhoods and make it financially viable to produce an environmentally-friendly pattern of settlement. An environmentally-friendly pattern of settlement which is sustainable in the sense that it is seen to guard the communities undergoing development (the said housing estate, village and neighbourhoods) against everything seen as a possible threat to them. That is the coalescence of settlements, loss of identity and break-up of communities which results from the pressure for infill development traditionally associated with peripheral expansion of this kind.

Its value, limitations and short-fallings

The value of the aesthetic may be seen to lie with its suggestion that it is possible for the model to design high quality living and working environments which are friendly. High quality living and working environments that are friendly because the land market upon which they rest produces enough planning gain to efficiently green the economic development in question and make it financially viable. That is efficiently green the economic development of the regeneration programme, town centre expansion and new neighbourhoods, make it financially viable and in turn produce an environmentally-friendly pattern of settlement.

If this is where the value of the aesthetic lies - and it certainly appears to be - then both its limitations and short-fallings need to be recognised. What needs to be recognised is that in its current form the model is unable to tell us whether the design of the high quality living and working environments which it advances are ecologically sound. Asking whether the high quality living and working environments are friendly because they are ecologically sound, or if it is due to the fact the land market produces enough planning gain to efficiently green the economic development of the estate, village and neighbourhoods and make it financially viable, exposes the limitations of the model and design solution it puts forward. It shows that in its current form, the model is only able to address one of the questions and not the other. It illustrates that the design can not tell us whether the high quality living and working environments are friendly because they are ecologically sound, only if the land market produces enough planning gain to efficiently green the economic development in question and make it financially viable.

Ecologically sound and efficient?

The question is perhaps, whether it is an answer to the former, or latter question which has the right to make claims about the environmentally-friendly nature of the settlement pattern? With the former - even though the model does not raise them - the questions are to do with the site's ecological footprint, bio-diversity and

Chapter 9

Conclusions

This book has examined the development of property management in terms of the corporate strategies and financial instruments made use of to appraise the land and buildings making up the urban environment.

The chapter on property management began by outlining the issues underlying the development of property management. Under the heading of: value for money, economy, efficiency and effectiveness, it drew attention to the corporate strategies and financial instruments of property management. From here the text went on to examine the corporate strategies developed to improve the standards of property management. It then went on to examine the financial instruments that have also been developed to bring about better standards of property management. Having set out the corporate strategies and financial instruments of property management, the examination turned attention to one of the most pressing issues facing the development of property management. Under the heading of 'computer-based information systems, property management and the appraisal of the urban environment', attention was drawn to how the corporate strategies and financial instruments in question, provide the capital accounting systems, asset registers and valuation methodologies needed to undertake a comprehensive appraisal of the land and buildings making up the urban environment. This examination showed that while a great deal of information is currently available on the various initiatives underlying the development of property management, there is still a noticeable absence of any data on either the corporate strategies, financial instruments, or computer-based information systems forming the mainstay of the capital accounting systems, asset registers and valuation methodologies under consideration. The examination has aimed to close the gap that currently exists in what is understood about the development of property management and do this by providing academics, middle managers, directors and chief executives, with the information required to not only manage property as a corporate resource, but make sure the strategies made use of for such purposes are financially sound.

Developing this theme, the examination went on to investigate the contribution capital accounting systems, asset registers and valuation methodologies make to sustainable urban development (SUD). Here the examination provided a framework for analysing SUD and a directory of the environmental assessment methods currently available to appraise land and buildings. Examining the assessment methods under the heading of 'valuation and investment appraisal', the examination went on to study the impact discounting; obsolescence and depreciation have on the urban environment. This study was then drawn upon to how the discounting mechanism is being used to develop sustainable communities.

Taking a multi-disciplinary approach to the developments, the examination has brought together two disciplines (property management and environmental science) which have previously remained separate fields of study. The first five chapters have focused attention on the development of property management. Here attention was drawn to the corporate strategies, financial instruments and computer-based information systems underlying the development of property management. However, it is also here - with the development of computer-based information systems - that the common ground underlying the development was seen to emerge. The common ground developed further in chapter six, where attention was drawn to the contribution capital accounting systems, asset registers and valuation methodologies make to SUD. From here on the gap that previously existed between property management and environmental science was bridged. Having bridged the gap, the text went on to develop the connection between the two disciplines. This was done by providing a framework for analysing SUD and a directory of the environmental assessment methods currently available to appraise land and buildings. Here the language, vocabulary and terms of reference linking both fields of study were introduced to highlight the relationship developing between property management and environmental science.

The examinations have gone some way to highlight the degree of change property management has recently been subject. Looked at together there can be little doubt the changes highlighted in the examination are significant and mark major developments in the field of property management. What-is-more, as landmark developments, the changes can also be seen as representative of the on-going commitment by academics, middle managers, directors and chief executives alike, to make property management more progressive, able in that sense to link with other fields of study which it is connected to.

The benefits of taking a multi-disciplinary approach to the developments and bringing together disciplines which have previously remained separate fields of study are numerous. They may be summarised as follows:

• it allows an examination of the core values underlying the development and issues lying at the centre of property management. This in turn allows attention to focus on the corporatisation of property management and the authority this gives central units to develop the financial instruments of capital accounting;

• the subsequent examination of the asset registers and valuation methodologies making up the financial instruments in question, draws attention to the computer-based information systems developed to appraise the land and buildings making up the urban environment. This examination of the information systems underlying the appraisal of land and buildings (and making up the urban environment) demonstrates the link between property management and environmental science. It illustrates the link is both corporate and financial and connected through the information systems developed to appraise the land and buildings making up the urban environment;

- the examination also shows that in order to be meaningful, the connection which exists between the two disciplines needs to be developed through a common language, set of vocabularies and shared terms of reference. It has been shown that it is SUD which provides the said language, vocabularies and terms of reference and advances a framework for analysing the sustainability of urban development. The framework of analysis that in turn provides the directory of environmental assessment methods available to assess the sustainability of urban development;
- classified in terms of environmental and sustainability (environmental, economic and social) assessments, the directory illustrates the significance of the valuation methodologies and investment appraisal techniques underlying the discounting mechanism adopted for such assessments. This in turn illustrates the significance of valuation and investment appraisal as financial instruments of the discounting mechanism and its appraisal of the land and buildings making up the urban environment. It also makes it possible to highlight the significant role the said mechanism plays in assessing not only the environmental, but economic and social sustainability of urban development. This in turn draws attention to the ecological, economic and social components of such assessments and the challenges this poses for the development of sustainable communities.

In holding such values, property management is seen to be progressive and committed to developing links with other fields of study which it is connected to. Likewise, in forging these links and strengthening the connection between property management and environmental science, the subject is seen to develop an inter-disciplinary nature. There can be little doubt the progressive, inter-disciplinary nature of the relationship between the two disciplines, ensures that property management does not develop in isolation from one of the few sciences it is linked to and shares a connection with. In linking property management with environmental science and forging a connection between the two disciplines, it is obvious that a wide-ranging set of opportunities open up for the academics, middle managers, directors and chief executives who have committed themselves to developing such relationships.

With the development of property management along the lines of corporate strategies and financial instruments, the benefits are primarily organisational and technical. With the development of the information systems needed to appraise the land and buildings making up the urban environment, the benefits are wider. They lie in the direct link the corporate strategies and financial instruments are able - by way of the information systems - to make with the range of environmental, economic and social policies governing urban development. The range of polices which in this instance make up the search for SUD and assessments that this in turn requires. However, while providing considerable opportunity for property management to become concerned with not only organisational and technical matters, but also issues related to environmental, economic and social policy, it should also be recognised this in turn raises a number of challenges. The challenges this raises are as follows:

- the need for property management to develop a working knowledge of the languages, vocabularies and terms of reference surrounding SUD and its framework for analysis. This requires that the technical and economic initiatives supporting the developing information systems and underlying both the corporate strategies and financial instruments of property management, require be supplemented with their equivalent environmental innovations. In view of the fact such a development requires the initiatives in question to be both technical, economic and environmental, it is evident this will change the informational basis of property management. However, what is not so clear is how the development will affect the process of corporatisation. The question that remains is how the said developments will affect the corporate strategies adopted for managing property. As the values of property management are now organisational, technical and policy-related, it is questionable whether the corporate strategies currently in existence are able to accommodate the environment within its current culture. The current culture is pro-quality, enterprise-minded, competitive, decentred, accountable and corporate. How the technology and economics of this can be balanced with the environmental is not clear. In many respects this question appears to have been 'put on hold' while attention turns to the matter of the valuation methodologies and investment appraisal techniques supporting the financial instruments of the development. However, as we have seen even here, the developments are far from straightforward, requiring capital accounting systems that are natural and social and which are based upon bio-physical and economic values. Recognising that over the past decade property management has given little attention to the former and has tended to concentrate on the latter, the extent of the challenge which recent developments pose starts to become evident. This is because to a large degree, the developments examined in chapters six, seven and eight of this book, represent the exceptions to the rule. In that sense attempts made by committed parties to not only link with environmental science, but also forge connections which contribute to the sustainability of urban development;
- the technical challenges of linking the environment and economy in a form of environmental economics able to deliver SUD have been documented in chapters six, seven and eight. As chapter six suggests, the technical issues associated with the development of environmental economics are considerable. However, as chapters seven and eight go some way to demonstrate, the difficulties these issues pose can be overcome and significant contributions commercial standards of this type can be made to make urban development sustainable.

One question that still remains relates to how the aforesaid will reallocate resources and which model of service provision should be adopted for such an 'environmentally-sensitive' reorganisation of property management? Whether, that is, the reforms which such developments usher in should be those of: 'cutting and reshaping', ' improving responsiveness' and the 'empowerment of the consumer'.

With the demise of privatisation and shift of policy towards sustainable development, it is difficult to see how the focus of attention should be on the cutting and reshaping of expenditure - unless of course the expenditure in question is producing environmental damage. In view of this, it is perhaps more likely that any reallocation of resources will be delivered through attempts to improve the responsiveness of property management to the demands for higher environmental standards and to empower the consumer in the process of making urban development sustainable.

In many respects, it may be argued that the re-organisation and reform property management has recently been subject to provides the platform needed for it to link with environmental science and address the technical challenges this poses. Why? Because both disciplines are currently undergoing a series of changes brought about in response to the search for SUD. This is clearly evident in the on-going debate about the use of valuation methodology and investment appraisal techniques in environmental assessment. The accounting systems that are being used to transcend the limitations of environmental valuations are based on investment appraisal techniques which employ discounting mechanisms as part of their sustainability assessments. The contribution that techniques of this kind make to such assessments is notable. They are notable and stand out for the fact this transformation of environmental assessment leads towards forms of urban development which can be said to be sustainable in not only environmental, but also economic and social terms. However, as chapter eight has pointed out, the use of such techniques to develop sustainable communities is fraught with difficulties and requires to undergo further development before such assessments can be seen the be both ecologically sound and economically efficient. The need to improve the responsiveness of property management to this environmental challenge and empower the consumer in this process of SUD, is perhaps still one of the main issues requiring further attention.

Appendix

List of Assessment Methods (19 September 2000)

Analysis of Interconnected Decision Areas (Aida)
Analytic Hierarchy Process (AHP)
ATHENA
BEPAC
BRE Environmental Assessment Method (BREEAM)
BRE Environmental Management Toolkits
Building Energy Environment (BEE 1.0)

Building Environmental Assessment and Rating System (BEARS)

Building for Economic and Environmental Sustainability (BEES 2:0)

Cluster Evaluation
Community Impact Evaluation
Concordance Analysis
Contingent Valuation Method
Cost Benefit Analysis
Eco-Effect

Eco-Indicator '95

Eco-Instal

Economic Impact Assessment
Ecological Footprint
Eco-points
Ecopro
Eco-Profile
EcoProP
Eco-Quantum
ENVEST
Environmental Impact Analysis

Environmental Impact Assessment

Environmental Profiles (The BRE Methodology for Environmental Profiles of Construction Materials, Components and Building Materials)
EQUER

ESCALE

Financial Evaluation of Sustainable Communities
Flag Model

Green Building Challenge

Green Guide to Specification: an Environmental Profiling System for Building
    Materials and Components

Hedonic analysis

Hochbaukonstruktionen nach ökologischen Gesichtspunkten (SIA D0123)

INSURED

Leadership in Energy and Environmental Design Green Building Rating System
    (LEEDTM)

Life Cycle Analysis (LCA)

Mass Intensity Per Service Unit (MIPS)

MASTER Framework

Meta Regression Analysis

Multi-Criteria Analysis

Net Annual Return Model

Optimierung der Gesamtanforderungen (Kosten/Energie/Umwelt) ein Instrument
    für die Integrale Planung (OGIP)

PAPOOSE

PIMWAQ

Project Impact Assessment

Planning Balance Sheet Analysis

Quantitative City Model

Regime Analysis

Risk Assessment Method(s)

SANDAT

Semantic Differential

Social Impact Assessment

SPARTACUS

Strategic Environmental Assessment (SEA)

SUDECIR

Sustainable cities

Sustainable communities

Sustainable regions

SYSTIM

Transit-orientated settlement

Travel cost theory

Bibliography

Adair, A. and McGreal, S. (1987), 'The Application of Multiple Regression Analysis in Property Valuation', *Journal of Valuation*, Vol. 6 (1), pp. 57-67.

Allwinkle, S. and Speed, C. (1997), 'Sustainability and the Built Environment: Tourism Impacts', in Brandon, P., Lombardi, P. and Bentivegna V. (eds), *Evaluation in the Built Environment for Sustainability*, E&FN Spon, London.

Altfield, R. and Dell, K. (1996), *Values, Conflict and The Environment*, Ashgate, Aldershot.

Arnison, C., Bibby, H. and Mulquinney, L. (1990), *Commercial Property Management*, Shaw and Sons, London.

Association of District Councils (1990a), *Property Management in District Councils - A Good Practice Guide*, ADC, London.

Association of District Councils (1990b), *Efficiency in Welsh District Councils - Property Management*, ADC, London.

Association of District Councils (1990c), *Property Management in District Councils - A Good Practice Guide*, ADC, London.

Audit Commission (1988a), *Local Authority Property - A Management Overview*, HMSO, London.

Audit Commission (1988b), *Local Authority Property - A Management Handbook*, HMSO, London.

Audit Commission (1988c), *Management Paper No.7*, HMSO, London.

Audit Commission (1988d), *Management Paper No.7*, HMSO, London.

Audit Commission (2000), *Hot Property*, HMSO, London.

Avis, M. and Gibson, V. (1995), *Real Estate Resource Management*, DTI, London.

Avis, M., Crosby, N., French, N. and Gibson, V. (1993), *Property Management Performance Monitoring*, GTI Oxford Brooks, Oxford.

Avis, M., Gibson, V. and Watts, J. (1989), *Managing Operational Property Assets*, Department of Land Management, Reading University.

Bains, M. (1972), *The New Local Authorities: Management and Structure*, HMSO London.

Balchin, P., Bull, G., Kieve, L. (1995), *Urban Land Economics and Public Policy*, Macmillan, London.

Banister, D. and Burton, K. (1993), *Transport, the Environment and Sustainable Development*, E&FN Spon, London.

Banner, G. (1988), 'Management Development in Public Administration: How to Meet the Challenge', in Brovetto, P., Holzer, R. and Kakabadse, A. (eds) *Management Development and the Public Sector - A European Perspective*, Gower, Aldershot.

Baum, A. (1989), 'A Critical Examination of the Measurement of Property Investment Risk', *Department of Land Economy, Discussion Paper No 22*, University of Cambridge.

Baum, A. (1991), *Property Investment, Depreciation and Obsolescence*, Routledge, London.

Baum, A. and Crosby, N. (1988), *Property Investment Appraisal*, Routledge, London.

Baum, A. and Crosby, N. (1995), *Property Investment Appraisal*, Routledge, London.

Baum, A. and Mackmin, D. (1989), *The Income Approach to Property Valuation*, Routledge, London.

Baum, A., Macgregor, B. (1992), 'The Initial Yield Revealed', *Journal Of Property Valuation And Investment*, Vol. 10 (4), pp. 709-726.

Beatley, T. (1995), 'Planning and Sustainability: The Elements of a New (Improved?) Paradigm', *Journal of Planning Literature*, Vol. 9 (4).

Bentivenga V. (1997), 'Limitations in Environmental Evaluations', in Brandon P., Lombardi, P. and Bentivegna, V. (eds), *Evaluation in the Built Environment for Sustainability*, E&FN Spon, London.

Bergh, J., Button, K., Nijkamp, P. and Pepping, G. (1997), *Meta-Analysis of Environmental Policies*, Klewer, Dordrecht.

Birtles, T. (1997), 'Environmental Impact Evaluation of Buildings and Cities for Sustainability', in Brandon, P., Lombardi, P. and Bentivegna, V. (eds), *Evaluation of the Built Environment for Sustainability*, Chapman and Hall, London.

Bizarro, F. and Nijkamp, P. (1997), 'Integrated Conservation of Cultural Built Heritage', in Brandon, P., Lombardi, P. and Bentivegna, V. (eds), *Evaluation of the Built Environment for Sustainability*, E&FN Spon, London.

Boyle, C. (1984), 'An Expert System of Valuation of Residential Properties', *Journal of Valuation*, Vol. 2, (3), pp. 271-286.

Brandon, P. and Lombardi, P. (2001), 'Structuring the Problem of Urban Sustainability for Holistic Decision Making', in *Proceedings of the First International Virtual Congress on Ecology and the City*, UPC, Departament de Construccions Arquitectoniques, Barcellona, March 2001 (http://www2.upc.es/ciec/).

Brandon, P., Lombardi, P. and Bentivenga, V. (1997), 'Introduction', in Brandon, P., Lombardi, P. and Bentivegna, V. (eds), *Evaluation of the Built Environment for Sustainability*, E&FN Spon, London.

Brandon, P., Lombardi, P., and Bentivegna, V. (1997), *Evaluation of the Built Environment for Sustainability*, E&FN Spon, London.

Breheny, M. (1992a), 'The Compact City', *Built Environment*, Vol. 18 (4), pp. 241-246.

Breheny, M. (1992b), *Sustainable Development and Urban Forms*, Pion, London.

Breheny, M. and Rookwood, R. (1993), 'Planning The Sustainable City Region', in Blowers, A. (ed) *Planning for a Sustainable Environment*, Earthscan Publications Ltd, London.

Breheny, M. and Rookwood, R. (1993), 'Planning the Sustainable City-Region', in Blowers, A. (ed), *Planning for a Sustainable Environment*, Earthscan, London.

Breheny, M. and Rookwood, R. (1993), 'Planning the Sustainable City Region', in Blowers, A. (ed), *Planning for a Sustainable Environment*, Earthscan Publications Ltd, London.

Breheny, M., Gent, T. and Lock, D. (1993), *Alternative Development Patterns: New Settlements*, HMSO, London.

Brehney, M. (1995), 'Counter-Urbanisation and Sustainable Urban Forms', in Brotchie, J. (ed), *Cities in Competition*, Longman, Melbourne.

Britton, W., Connellan, O. and Crofts, M. (1991), *The Cost Approach to Valuation*, School of Surveying, Kingston Polytechnic and Surrey County Council, Kingston-upon-Thames.

Britton, W., Connellan, O. and Crofts, M. (1989), *The Economic, Efficient and Effective Management of Public Sector Landed Estates*, Kingston University, Surrey County Council, Kingston-upon-Thames.

Brooks, C., Cheshire, A., Evans, A. and Stabler, M. (1997), 'The Economic and Social Value of the Conservation of Historic Buildings and Areas', in Brandon, P., Lombardi, P. and Bentivegna, V., *Evaluation of the Built Environment for Sustainability*, E&FN Spon, London.

Brooks, C., Cheshire, P., Evans, A. and Stabler, M. (1997), 'The Economic and Social Value of the Conservation of Historic Buildings and Areas: Economics of Conservation', in Brandon, P., Lombardi, P. and Bentivenga, V. (eds) *Evaluation of the Built Environment for Sustainability*, Chapman and Hall, London.

Brown, F. (1998), 'Modelling Urban Growth', *Town and Country Planning*, November, pp. 334-337.

Brown, G. (1991), *Property Investment and the Capital Markets*, Chapman and Hall, London.

Brown, R. and Arnold, A. (1993), *Managing Corporate Real Estate*, John Wiley and Sons, New York.

Butt, H. and Palmer, D. (1985), *Value for Money in the Public Sector*, Macmillan, London.

Byrne, P. (1992), *Local Government in Britain*, Penguin, London.

Byrne, T. (1995), *Risk, Uncertainty and Decision Making in Property Development*, E&F Spon, London.

Campbell, S. (1996), 'Green Cities, Growing Cities, just Cities?', *Journal of the American Planning Association*, Vol. 62 (4).

Capello R., Nijkamp P. and Pepping, G. (1999), *Sustainable Cities and Energy Policies*, Springer-Verlag, Berlin.

Carter, E. (1999), 'Evaluating Property Performance', in Deakin (ed), *Local Authority Property Management: Initiatives, Strategies, Re-organisation and Reform*, Ashgate Press, Aldershot.

CEC - Commission of The European Community, European's Fifth Environmental Action Programme (1993), *Toward Sustainability*, CEC, Brussels.

CEC (1998), *Sustainable Urban Development in the European Union - A Framework for Action*, CEC Brussels.

Chambers, D. (1988), 'Learning from Markets', *Public Money and Management*, Vol. 8 (4), pp. 47-50.

Chandler, J. (1991), 'Public Administration and Private Management - Is there a Difference?', *Public Administration*, Vol. 9 (3), pp. 385-392.

Chartered Institute of Public Finance and Accountancy (1989), *Capital Accounting in Local Authorities - The Way Forward*, CIPFA, London.

Chartered Institute of Public Finance and Accountancy (1991a), *CIPFA Statement - Capital Accounting in Local Authorities*, CIPFA, London.

Chartered Institute of Public Finance and Accountancy (1991b), *Asset Registers*, CIPFA, London.

Chartered Institute of Public Finance and Accountancy (1992a), *Capital Accounting by Local Authorities - Report of the Implementation Studies*, CIPFA, London.

Chartered Institute of Public Finance and Accountancy (1992b), *Directory of Asset Management Software*, CIPFA, London.

Chartered Institute of Public Finance and Accountancy (1994), *Asset Registers: An Update*, CIPFA, London.

Chesterton (1996), '*Edinburgh's South-East Wedge*', in 'Final IDF Document', Chesterton Consulting, London.

Clark, S. (1988), 'Local Authority Property Management', in Hillier Parker (ed) *Hillier Parker Occasional Papers*, Hillier Parker, London.

Cloakley, J. (1994), 'The Integration of Property and Financial Markets', *Environment and Planning A*, Vol. 26, pp. 697-713.

Cochrane, A. (1993), *Whatever Happened to Local Government?*, OU Press, Buckingham.

Cole, R. (1997), 'Prioritising Environmental Criteria in Building Design', in Brandon, P. et al, *Evaluation Of The Built Environment for Sustainability*, Chapman and Hall, London.

Common, R., Flynn, N. and Melloun, E. (1993), *Managing Public Services*, Butterworth-Heineman, Oxford.

Connellan, O. (1994), 'Discounted Asset Rent (DAR) - "A New Methodology for Cost Appraisals"', *Journal of Property Valuation and Investment*, Vol. 12 (4).

Connellan, O. (1997), 'Valuation of Specialised Public Sector Assets', *Property Management*, Vol. 15, (4).

Connellan, O. and Baldwin, M. (1992), 'The Cost Approach to Valuation', *Journal of Property Valuation and Investment*, Vol. 11 (1), pp. 50-55.

Cooper, I. (1999), 'Which Focus for Building Assessment Methods?', *Building Research and Information*, Vol. 27 (4).

Cooper, I. (1997), 'Environmental Assessment Methods for Use at the Building and City Scale: Constructing Bridges or Identifying Common Ground', in Brandon, P. et al, *Evaluation of the Built Environment For Sustainability*, Chapman and Hall, London.

Cooper, I. (1999), 'Which Focus for Building Assessment Methods?', *Building Research and Information*, Vol. 27 (4/5), pp. 321-331.

Cooper, I. (2000), 'Inadequate Grounds for a "Design-Led" Approach to Urban Design', *Building Research and Information*, Vol. 28, (3), pp. 212-219.

Cooper, I. and Curwell, S. (1998), 'The Implications of Urban Sustainability', *Building Research and Information*, Vol. 26 (1), pp. 17-28.

Cosgriff, B. and Steinemann, A. (1998), 'Industrial Ecology for Sustainable Communities', *Journal of Environmental Planning and Management*, Vol. 41 (6).

Crofts, M. (1989), 'Public Land Management - Land Audits and Asset Rents', *Estates Gazette*, 8928, pp. 66-70.

Curwell, S. and Lombardi, P. (1999), 'Riqualificazione Urbana Sostenibile', *Urbanistica*, (112), giugno 1999, pp. 96-103 (English version, pp. 114-115).

Curwell, S., Hamilton, A. and Cooper, I. (1998), 'The BEQUEST Network: Towards Sustainable Urban Development', *Building Research and Information*, Vol. 26 (1), pp. 56-65.

Curwell, S., Yates, A., Howard, N., Bordass, B. and Doggart, J. (1999), 'The Green Building Challenge in the UK', *Building Research and Information*, Vol. 27 (4/5), pp. 286-293.

Czernkowski, R. (1990), 'Expert Systems in Real Estate Valuation', *Journal of Valuation*, Vol. 8, (4), pp. 376-393.

Davoudi, S. (1997), 'Economic Development and Environmental Gloss: New Structure Plan for Lancashire', in Brandon, P., Lombardi, P. and Bentivenga, V, (ed), *Evaluation of the Built Environment for Sustainability*, Chapman and Hall, London.

Deakin, M. (1998d), 'How Effectively do Local Authorities Manage their Property Assets?', *Research Report No.23*, RICS, London.

Deakin, M. (1994), 'Initial Considerations on the Cost Approach', *Cutting Edge*, RICS, London.

Deakin, M. (1995), 'The Development of Financial Services for the Property Management Divisions of Kiev City', in *Our Common Estates Series*, RICS, London.

Deakin, M. (1996), 'Discounting, Obsolescence, Depreciation and their Effects on the Environment of Cities', *Journal of Financial Management of Property and Construction*, Vol. 1 (2), pp. 39-57.

Deakin, M. (1997a), 'The Development of Computer-based Information Systems for Local Authority Property Management: The Underlying Issues', *Journal of Financial Management of Property and Construction*, Vol. 2 (1), pp. 59-83.

Deakin, M. (1997b), 'The Development of Computer-based Information Systems for Local Authority Property Management: The Application', *Journal of Financial Management of Property and Construction*, Vol. 2 (2), pp. 57-74.

Deakin, M. (1997c), 'An Economic Evaluation and Appraisal of the Effects Land Use, Building Obsolescence and Depreciation have on the Environment of Cities', in Brandon, P., Lombardi, P. and Bentivenga, V. (eds) *Evaluation of the Built Environment for Sustainability*, Chapman and Hall, London.

Deakin, M. (1998a), 'The Development of Computer-Based Information Systems for Local Authority Property Management', *Property Management*, Vol. 16 (2), pp. 61-82.

Deakin, M. (1998b), *The Development of Local Authority Property Management*, RICS, London.

Deakin, M. (1998c), *The Development of Local Authority Property Management*, (http://www.rics.org.uk.research/download/index.html).

Deakin, M. (1998e), 'How Effectively do Local Authorities Manage their Property Assets?', *Chartered Surveyor Monthly*, May.

Deakin, M. (1998f), 'Local Authority Property Management: A Management Exercise', *Journal of Financial Management of Property and Construction*, Vol. 3 (1), pp. 43-71.

Deakin, M. (1998g), 'Effective Local Authority Property Management', Paper presented to the meeting of the Association of Chief Estates Surveyors (ACES), Department of Environment, Transport and the Regions, London.

Deakin, M. (1999a), 'Financial Instruments for Capital Accounting', *Journal of Property Investment And Finance*, Vol. 17, (1), pp. 89-107.

Deakin, M. (1999b), 'The Underlying Issues, Aims, Model and Post-AC Studies', in Deakin (ed), *Local Authority Property Management: Initiatives, Strategies, Re-organisation and Reform*, Ashgate Press, Aldershot.

Deakin, M. (1999c), 'The Development of Local Authority Property Management', in Deakin (ed), *Local Authority Property Management: Initiatives, Strategies, Re-organisation and Reform*, Ashgate Press, Aldershot.

Deakin, M. (1999d), 'Local Authority Property Management: The Underlying Issues, Model and Task Ahead', *Cutting Edge*, RICS, London.

Deakin, M. (1999e), 'The Development of Local Authority Property Management: The Search for the All-Pervasive Market', *Real Estate Valuation and Investment*, Vol. 3 (1), pp. 23-46.

Deakin, M. (1999f), 'Valuation, Appraisal, Discounting, Obsolescence and Depreciation: Towards a Life Cycle Analysis and Impact Assessment of their Effects on the Environment of Cities', *International Journal of Life Cycle Assessment*, Vol. 4 (2), pp. 87-94.

Deakin, M. (2000a), 'Property Asset Management: Towards a Pro-Investment Form, *Journal of Financial Management of Property and Construction*, Vol. 5 (1/2), pp. 15-32.

Deakin, M. (2000b), 'Developing Sustainable Communities in Edinburgh's South East Wedge, *Journal of Property Management*, Vol. 4 (4), pp. 72-87.

Deakin, M. (2000c), *The Transition to Property Management*, Chandos Publishing, Oxford.

Deakin, M. (2002a), *The Transition to Property Management*, Estates Gazette, London.

Deakin, M. (2002b), Modelling the Development of Sustainable Communities in Edinburgh's South East Wedge, *Planning Practice and Research*, Vol. 17 (4), pp. 331-336.

Deakin, M. and Curwell, S. (2002c), 'Sustainable Urban Development and BEQUEST', *Building Research and Information*, 30 (2), pp. 79-82.

Dent, P. (1997), 'Managing Public Sector Property Assets: Valuation Issues', *Property Management*, Vol. 15 (4).

Dent, P. and Bond, S. (1992), 'Public Property Holdings: Evaluating the Assets', *Property Management*, Vol. 11 (4), pp. 314-318.

Dent, P. and Bond, S. (1992), 'Public Property Holdings: Evaluating the Assets', *Property Management*, Vol. 11, (4), pp. 314-318.

Department Of Environment (1991), *Project Appraisal*, HMSO, London.

Dixon, T. (1985), 'Computer Software Availability for Valuation', *Journal of Valuation*, Vol. 4 (4), pp. 21-32.

Dixon, T. (1989), *Computerised Information Systems for Surveyors*, Surveyors Publications, London.

Dixon, T. (1995), *Using Microcomputers for Property Valuation and Appraisal*, CEM, Reading.

Dixon, T., Hargitay, S. and Bevan, O. (1991), *Microcomputers in Property: a Surveyor's Guide to Lotus 1-2-3 and dBase IV*, Spon, London.

Dobson, S. and Rosemary, S. (1990), 'Public and Private Sector Management: the Case for a Wider Debate', *Public Money and Management*, Vol. 10 (1), pp. 37-40.

DoE. (1991), *Policy Appraisal and the Environment*, HMSO, London.

DoE. (1993a), *The Effectiveness of Green Belts*, HMSO, London.

DoE. (1993b), *Reducing Transport Emissions through Planning*, HMSO, London.

DoE. (1993c), *Environmental Appraisal of Development Plans*, HMSO, London.

DoE. (1993d), *Making Markets Work for the Environment*, HMSO, London.

DoE. (1994), *Guide on Preparing Environmental Statements for Planning Projects* [draft], HMSO, London.

DoE. (1998), *Environmental Assessment* [Circular 15/88] HMSO, London.

Dubourg, R. and Pearce, D. (1997), 'Paradigms for Environmental Choice: Sustainability Versus Optimality', in Faucheaux, S., Pearce, D., Proops, J. (eds), *Models of Sustainable Development*, Edward Elgar, Cheltenham.

Edington, G. (1997), *Property Management - A Customer Focused Approach*, Macmillan, London.

Edward Erdman (1992), *Property Asset Registers - A National Survey of the Local Authority Response to Implementation*, Edward Erdman, London.

Elcock, H. (1994), *Local Government*, Routledge, London.

Faucheaux, S. and O'Conner, M. (1998), 'Introduction', in Faucheaux, S., O'Conner, M. (eds) *Valuation For Sustainable Development*, Edward Elgar, Cheltenham.

Fisher, I. (1965), *The Theory of Interest*, Augustus, M. Kelly, New York (Fourth Edition).

French, N. (1994), 'Asset Registers and Asset Rents for Local Authorities: A Viable Property Management Tool', *Property Management*, Vol. 12, (3).

French, N. and Hague, L. (1999), 'Local Authority Property: Asset Registers, Valuation and Property Audits', in Deakin, M. (ed), *Local Authority Property Management: Initiatives, Strategies, Re-organisation and Reform*, Ashgate Press, Aldershot.

Fusco, L. and Nijkamp P. (1997), *Le Valutazioni per lo Sviluppo Sostenibile della Città e del Territorio*, Angeli, Milan.

Gammons, J. (1990), 'Property Rationalisation - a Local Authority Initiative' *Property Management*, Vol. 8 (1), pp. 23-27.

Gibbs, D., Longhurst, J. and Braithwaite, C. (1996), 'Moving Towards Sustainable Development: Integrating Economic Development and the Environment in Local Authorities', *Journal of Environmental Planning and Management*, Vol. 39 (3).

Gibson, V. (1986), 'A Management View of Valuation in Information Technology' *Journal of Valuation*, Vol. 5 (1), pp. 30-40.

Gibson, V. (1991), 'Who Can Manage Property Best: The Private or Public Sector?', *Property Management*, Vol. 9 (1).

Gibson, V. (1994), 'Strategic Property Management: How Can Local Authorities Develop a Property Strategy?', *Property Management*, Vol. 12 (3), pp. 9-15.

Gibson, V. (1995), 'Is Property on the Strategic Agenda?' *Property Review*, Vol. 5 (1), pp. 104-109.

Gibson, V. and Carter, E. (1996), 'Is Property on the Strategic Agenda?', *Chartered Surveyor Monthly*, January.

Glasson, J., Therival, R. and Chadwick, A. (1994), *Environmental Impact Assessment*, University College, London.

Gordon, G. (1982), 'Reported In Bingham, E.', in *Financial Management: Theory and Practice*, Dryden Press, Chicago.

Graham, S. and Marvin, S. (1996), *Telecommunications and the City*, Routledge, London.

Greaves, M. (1984), 'The Determinants of Residential Values', *Journal of Valuation*, Vol. 3 (1), pp. 271-286.

Grillenzoni, M., Ragazzoni, G., Bazzani, G. and Canavari, M. (1997), 'Land Planning and Resource Evaluation for Public Investments', in Brandon, P., Lombardi, P. and Bentivegna, V. *Evaluation of the Built Environment for Sustainability*, E&FN Spon, London.

Gronow, S., Scott, I. and Rosser, B. (1989), 'The Nature and Use of Uncertainty in Property Valuation Expert Systems', *Journal of Valuation*, Vol. 7 (3), pp. 218-247.

Guy, S. and Marvin, S. (1997), Splintering Networks: Cities and Technical Networks in 1990s Britain, *Urban Studies*, Vol. 34 (2), pp. 191-216.

Hall, P. and Ward, C. (1998), *Sociable Cities*, John Wiley, London.

Hambleton, R. (1989), 'Urban Government under Thatcher and Reagan', *Urban Affairs Quarterly*, Vol. 24 (3), pp. 359-88.

Hambleton, R. (1993), 'Consumerism, Decentralisation and Local Democracy', in Roberts, P., Struthers, T. and Sacks, T. (eds) *Managing the Metropolis*, Avebury Press, Aldershot.

Hambleton, R., Hoggett, P. and Nolan, F. (1989), 'The Decentralisation of Public Services: A Research Agenda', *Local Government Studies*, January/February, pp. 39-56.

Harou, P., Daly, H. and Goodland, R. (1994), 'Environmental Sustainability through Project Appraisal', *Sustainable Development*, Vol. 2 (3), pp. 13-21.

Harrow, J. and Willcocks, L. (1990), 'Risk and the Public Service Manager', *Public Money and Management*, Vol. 10 (3), pp. 61-4.

Harvey, J. (1989), *Urban Land Economics*, Macmillan, London.

Harvey, J. (1996), *Urban Land Economics*, Macmillan, London.

Haughton, G. and Hunter C. (1994), *Sustainable Cities*, Jessica Kingsley, London.

Headley, C., Rushforth, J. and Whealan, J. (1999), 'Estate Management Performance Measures for the Higher Education Sector', *Cutting Edge*, RICS, London.

Heald, D. and Scott, D. (1996), 'The Valuation of NHS Hospitals under Capital Charging', *Journal of Property Research*, Vol. 13 (4).

Henkel, M. (1991), 'The Audit Commission', in Pollitt, C. and Harrison, S. (eds) *Handbook of Public Services Management*, Blackwell, Oxford.

HM Government (1990), *This Common Inheritance* HMSO, London.

HM Government (1991), *This Common Inheritance* HMSO, London.

HM Government (1994a), *This Common Inheritance* HMSO, London.

HM Government (1994b), *Sustainable Development: The UK Strategy* HMSO, London.

Hoggett, P. (1987), 'A Farewell to Mass Production? Decentralisation as an Emergent Private and Public Sector Paradigm', in Hoggett, P. and Hambleton, R. (eds) *Decentralisation and Democracy: Localising Public Services*, School for Advanced Urban Studies, University of Bristol.

Hoggett, P. and Hambleton, R. (eds) (1987), *Decentralisation and Democracy: Localising Public Services*, School for Advanced Urban Studies, University of Bristol.

Hsia M. (1989), 'User-oriented Property Management Systems', *Property Management*, Vol 7. (4).

Hsia, M. and Byrne, P. (1989), 'Automated Property Performance Analysis: Considerations on the Development of a PC Based Information System Prototype', *Working Paper No 2, Land Management Department*, Reading University.

Institute of Directors (1991), *Director's Guide to Property*, IOD, London.

Jenkins, D. and Gronow, S. (1989), 'IT in Local Government Property Management', *Estates Gazette,* 8844.

Jenkins, D., Gronow, S. and Prescott, G. (1989), 'Information Technology - the Changing Nature of Local Government Property Management', *Property Management*, Vol. 8 (1).

Jones, P., Vaughan, N., Cooke, P. and Sutcliffe, A. (1997), 'An Energy and Environmental Prediction Model for Cities', in Brandon, P., Lombardi, P. and Bentivegna V., *Evaluation of the Built Environment for Sustainability*, E&FN Spon, London.

Joroff, M., Lovargand, M., Lambert, S. and Franklin, B. (1993), *Strategic Management of the Fifth Resource: Corporate Real Estate,* (Industrial Development Research Council), Massachusetts Institute of Technology, Cambridge MA.

Jowsey, E. and Kellett, J., 1996. 'Sustainability and Methodologies of Environmental Assessment for Cities', in Pugh, C., *Sustainability, the Environment and Urbanisation*, Earthscan Publications Ltd , London.

Kirkwood, J. (1984), *Information Technology and Land Administration*, Estates Gazette, London.

Kirkwood, J. and Padden, J. (1988), 'Property Management - what the Audit Commission did not Tell us!', *Estates Gazette*, 8842, pp. 24-28.

Kooiman, J. (1988), 'Public Management in Europe', in Brovetto, P., Holzer, R and Kakabadse, A. (eds), *Management Development and the Public Sector a European Perspective*, Gower, Aldershot.

Kozlowski, J. and Hill, J. (1993), *Towards Planning for Sustainable Development: A Guide or the Ultimate Threshold Method*, Avebury, Aldershot.

Lash, S. and Urry, J. (1987), *The End of Organized Capitalism*, Polity, Cambridge.

Lash, S. and Urry, J. (1994), *Economies of Signs and Space*, Sage, New York.

Leach, S., Stewart, J. and Walsh, K. (1994), *The Changing Organisation and Management of Local Government*, Macmillan, London.

Lichfield, N. (1996), *Community Impact Evaluation*, University College London, London.

Local Authority Valuers Association (1989), *Effective Property Management through Review*, LAVA, London.

Local Government Management Board (1994), *Greening Economic Development*, LGMB, Luton.

Lombardi, P. (2000), 'A Framework for Understanding Sustainability in the Cultural Built Environment', in Brandon, P.S., Lombardi, P. and Srinath, P. (eds), *Cities & Sustainability. Sustaining our Cultural Heritage*, Conference Proceedings, Vishva Lekha Sarvodaya, Sri Lanka, (4), pp.1-25.

Lombardi, P. (2001), 'Responsibilities toward the Coming Generation Forming a New Creed, *Urban Design Studies*, Vol. 7.

Lothian Regional Council (1995), *Structure Plan Review*, LRC, Edinburgh.

Management Analysis Centre (1985), *Competition and the Chartered Surveyor*, MAC, London.

Martindale, N. (1995), 'Local Authority Property Investment: A Virtual Reality', *Property Management*, Vol. 13 (1).

Martindale, N. (1997), 'Local Authority Non-Operational Property - Serviceable or Surplus', *Property Management*, Vol. 15 (2).

Marvin, S. and Guy, S. (1997), 'Infrastructure Provision, Development Process and the Co-Production of Environmental Value', *Urban Studies*, Vol. 34 (12), pp. 2023-2036.

Massam, B. (1988), 'Multi-Criteria Decision Making (MCDM) Techniques in Planning', *Progress in Planning*, Vol. 30, Part 1.

Maud (1969), *Report of the Committee on Management of Local Government*, HMSO, London.

May, A., Mitchell, G. and Kupiszewska, D. (1997), 'The Development of the Leeds Quantifiable City Model', in Brandon, P., Lombardi, P. and Bentivegna, V. (eds), *Evaluation of the Built Environment For Sustainability*, E&FN Spon, London.

Mazza, M. and Rydin, Y. (1997), 'Urban Sustainability: Discourses, Networks and Policy Tools', *Progress in Planning*, Vol. 47, Part 1.

McGuigan, J. (1996), *Culture and the Public Sphere*, Routledge, London.

Metcalfe, L. (1988), 'Accountable Public Management: UK Concepts and Experience', in Brovetto, P., Holzer, R. and Kakabadse, A. (eds) *Management Development and the Public Sector a European Perspective*, Gower, Aldershot.

Miltin, D. and Satterhwaite, D. (1996), 'Sustainable Development and Cities', in Pugh, C., *Sustainabilty, the Environment and Urbanisation*, Earthscan Publications Ltd, London.

Mitchell G. (1999), *A Geographical Perspective on the Development of Sustainable Urban Regions*, Earthscan.

Mitchell, G. (1996), Problems and Fundamentals of Indicators of Sustainable Development', *Sustainable Development*, Vol. 4 (1), pp. 1-11.

Mitchell, G., May, A. and Mcdonald, A. (1995), 'PICABUE: A Methodological Framework for the Development of Indicators of Sustainable Development', *International Journal of Sustainable Development World Ecology*, Vol. 2, pp. 104-123.

Mollart, R. (1988), 'Monte-Carlo Simulation Using LOTUS 1-2-3', *Journal of Property Valuation*, Vol. 6 (4), pp. 419-433.

Mollart, R. (1994), 'Using Lotus 1-2-3 for Risk Analysis', *Journal of Property Valuation and Investment*, Vol. 12 (3), pp. 89-96.

Nijkamp P. and Pepping, G. (1998), 'A Meta-Analytic Evaluation of Sustainable City Initiatives', *Urban Studies*, Vol. 35 (9), pp. 1439-1455.

Nijkamp, P. and Perrels, A. (1994), *Sustainable Cities in Europe: A Comparative Analysis of Urban Energy and Environmental Policies*, Earthscan, London.

Nijkamp, P. (1991), *Urban Sustainability*, Gower, Aldershot.

Nijkamp, P., Rietveld, P. and Voogd, H. (1990), *Multicriteria Evaluation in Physical Planning*, Elsevier, Amsterdam.

Norgaard, R. (1984), 'Coevloutionary Development Potential', *Land Economics*, Vol. 60, pp. 160-172.

Norgaard, R. and Howarth, R. (1991), 'Sustainability and Discounting the Future', in Costanza, R., *Ecological Economics*, Columbia University Press.

O' Brian, M., Doig, A. and Clift, R. (1996), 'Social and Environmental Life Cycle Assessment', *International Journal Of Life Cycle Assessment*, Vol. 1 (4), pp. 231-237.

O'Conner, M. (1998), 'Ecological-Economic Sustainability', in Faucheaux, S., O'Conner, M. (ed), *Valuation For Sustainable Development*, Edward Elgar, Cheltenham.

Palmer, J., Cooper, I. and van der Vost, R. (1997), 'Mapping Out Fuzzy Buzzwords - who Sits Where on Sustainability and Sustainable Development', *Sustainable Development*, Vol. 5 (2), pp. 87-93.

Pearce D. (1971), *Capital Investment Appraisal*, Macmillan, London.

Pearce D. and Turner R. (1990), *Economic of Natural Resources and the Environment*, Harvester Wheatsheaf, Hemel Hempstead.

Pearce, D. (1972), *Cost-Benefit Analysis*, Macmillan, London.

Pearce, D. and Markanya, A. (1989), *Environmental Policy Benefits: Monetary Valuation*, OECD, Paris.

Pearce, D. and Turner, R (1990), *Economics of Natural Resources and The Environment*, Harvester Wheatsheaf, London.

Pearce, D. and Warford, J. (1993), *World Without End: Economic, Environment and Sustainable Development*, Oxford University Press, Oxford.

Powell, J., Pearce, D. and Craighill, A. (1997), 'Approaches to Valuation in LCA Impact Assessment', *International Journal of Life Cycle Assessment*, Vol. 2 (1), pp. 11-15.

Prior, J. (1993), *Building Research Establishment Environment Assessment Method, BREEAM, Version 1/93, New Offices*, Building Research Establishment Report.

Pugh, C. (1996), 'Sustainability and Sustainable Cities', in Pugh, C., *Sustainability, the Environment and Urbanisation*, Earthscan Publications Ltd, London.

Ralphs, M. and Wyatt, P. (1999), 'The Application of Geographic and Land Information Systems to the Management of Local Authority Property Management', in Deakin (ed), *Local Authority Property Management: Initiatives, Strategies, Re-organisation and Reform*, Ashgate, Aldershot.

Ratcliffe, J. and Stubbs, M. (1996), *Urban Planning and Real Estate Development*, University College, London, London.

Rees, W. (1992), 'Ecological Footprints and Appropriated Carrying Capacity: What Urban Economics Leaves Out', *Environment and Urbanisation*, Vol. 4 (2), pp. 121-130.

Richardson, H., Vipond, J. and Furbey, R. (1975), *Housing and Urban Spatial Structure*, Saxon House, London.

Roberts, B. (1983), 'Property Management in a Local Authority', *Property Management* 1, Vol., 3, pp. 223-228.

Roberts, B. (1984), 'Managing the Corporate Estate of Leicester City Council', *Property Management*, Vol. 2 (3), pp. 198-205.

Royal Institution of Chartered Surveyors (1993), *Valuation Guidance Notes*, RICS, London.

Royal Institution of Chartered Surveyors (1995), *Appraisal and Valuation Manual*, RICS, London.

Rydin, Y. (1992), 'Environmental Impacts and the Property Market', in Breheny M. (ed), *Sustainable Development And Urban Form*, Earthscan Publications Ltd, London.

Rydin, Y. (1992), 'Environmental Impacts and the Property Market', in Breheny M. (ed), *Sustainable Development and Urban Form*, Earthscan Publications Ltd, London.

Salway, F. (1986), *Depreciation Of Commercial Property*, CALUS, Reading.

Scarrett, D. (1983), *Property Management*, E&FN Spon, London.

Scarrett, D. (1995), *Property Asset Management*, E&FN Spon, London.

Scottish Office. (1994), *Setting Forth: Environmental Appraisal of Alternative Strategies*, Edinburgh.

Selman, P. (1996), *Local Sustainability*, Sage, London.

Society of Local Authority Chief Executives. (1986), *Our Heritage - Property Management in a Local Authority*, SOLACE, London.

Spicer, J. (1979), *Property Information Systems for Government*, DOE, London.

Stapleton, T. (1986), *Estate Management Practice*, Estates Gazette, London.

Stapleton, T. (1994), *Estate Management Practice*, Estates Gazette, London.